Priority One

EP BOOKS
Faverdale North
Darlington
DL3 0PH, England

web: http://www.epbooks.org

e-mail: sales@epbooks.org

EP Books are distributed in the USA by:
JPL Distribution
3741 Linden Avenue Southeast
Grand Rapids, MI–49548

First published 2013

British Library Cataloguing in Publication Data available

ISBN: 978–0–85234–935–9

Printed by Bell & Bain Ltd, Glasgow

For Nora Hooker and in memory of David Hooker
(18 April 1941–17 September 1993)—
my parents who taught me the 'first things' of the faith.

'It is always good to return to the gospel and, as Josh Hooker suggests in this excellent book, "to make it a daily discipline to return in our minds to the cross of Jesus. If we fail to remember God's grace shown to us each day then our lives will not be intentionally shaped by that grace." *Priority One* is a great tool to help us do just that, particularly showing us in some depth how the New Testament authors applied the gospel of grace to the situations facing various churches and believers. There is much here for twenty-first-century churches and individual Christians alike.'

Andy Lines
Mission Director
Crosslinks

'This is a fine treatment of the subject of grace, well grounded in doctrine, but eminently practical. It steers between the twin evils of legalism and lawlessness and is full of practical application. Diagrams help to make the message clear. I warmly recommend it.'

Robert Oliver

'The title of this short book is exactly right. There is no more important priority in the Christian life (in all of life, indeed) than the grace of God, the creator and redeemer of the universe. We need to seek God's grace not just at the moment of conviction and conversion, but every moment ever after. Unfortunately the church easily generates a culture of pretence or denial. There is an unholy paradox that in order to become a Christian and belong to the church the first thing you have to do is admit you're a failure in need of God's mercy and grace, but in order to "sustain your membership" as a respected member of the church, the last thing you should ever do is admit you're a failure. So we struggle on with inner guilt and shame, while our outward lives either stiffen with righteous rules or slacken with casual worldliness. Josh Hooker's book points a better way—indeed the only way: not only to start with the cross but to go on daily living in the power of the cross and the resurrection life that follows. Josh Hooker's book is thoroughly biblical in its approach, practical in application, rich in lively illustration, and full of encouragement and challenge in equal measure. As one of Josh's former teachers at All Nations Christian College, it is a joy to recommend this book.'

Christopher J. H. Wright
Langham Partnership

Acknowledgements

This manuscript has bounced electronically between Australia, Namibia and the United Kingdom. My thanks to Betty Flood who went beyond the call of duty as a mother-in-law in proof-reading my work. My thanks also to Peter and Paula Ryan for their comments and corrections which made the finished product much better than it would have been originally. The mistakes are all my own. My thanks also go to Evangelical Press for taking on this project.

No book is written in a vacuum and I am profoundly grateful to those who have faithfully taught me from God's Word over the years. Your names are too many to mention, but you know who you are and the contents of this book have been shaped by your teaching. In particular, I want to mention the influence of *World Harvest Mission* on me as a young pastor in setting me thinking along these lines about what it means to live by grace.

I would like to thank the staff and students of Namibia Evangelical Theological Seminary for the partnership I enjoy with them in proclaiming the message of God's grace.

I must acknowledge the role of Cathy, my wife and good

friend. She has encouraged me throughout the writing process and has read the manuscript at many different stages. My prayer for my children—Benjamin, Erin and Matthew—is that their lives would be gripped by this life-changing message.

As I have written the words that follow my prayer has been that God's people would be strengthened and encouraged. '… to the only wise God be glory for ever through Jesus Christ!' (Romans 16:27)

Contents

Introduction

A number of years ago I was asked to speak at the wedding of some friends who live in Scotland. The church they normally attended was not suitable for the wedding so they chose a picturesque church nearby for the service. When I arrived at the church I wandered up to the front to see where I would be speaking from. As I did so I was stopped by a man who introduced himself as 'the beadle'. When I explained that I would be preaching at the service he took me somewhat reluctantly to the lectern and asked me how long I would be speaking for. The couple who invited me had asked me to give just a short evangelistic sermon, conscious of the fact that there were many people at the wedding who were not Christians. So I told the beadle that I would be speaking for about ten to twelve minutes. (What I did not tell him was that this was probably one of the shortest Bible talks I had ever given.) He was clearly unimpressed by my answer. He replied curtly: 'Ten to twelve minutes? What on earth have you got to say that will take ten to twelve minutes?'

It was not clear whether the comment was aimed at the

sermon or the preacher, but it did make me wonder when the Christian message had last been heard in that church. It seemed that the beadle had no expectation of preaching with any real content. Maybe his idea of a wedding sermon was the telling of a few heart-warming stories, rather than teaching the Bible.

Certainly many today seem to promote a type of Christianity that has little room for teaching the Bible. However if we want to use the label 'Christian' of ourselves with any real integrity then we need to be *Bible people*. Sadly, we live at a time when many Christians have little knowledge of the Bible. We can quickly tell others the position of our football team in the league, or the latest story-line in our favourite TV soap, but if we were asked a basic question about biblical history or theology we would not be able to answer it. Many Christians do not know whether Daniel came before or after Joshua in Old Testament history, or what the New Testament means by 'justification'.

The beating heart of Christianity

In theory we know as Christians that the Bible is God's Living Word, but in practice we often live as if it is not. The truth is that we do not really know what it says and therefore it does not shape our lives in the way it should. We are a generation of Christians who have grown comfortable with a superficial understanding of the Bible that we have gained in passing from others. Our Bible knowledge is often second-hand. Even the most committed Christians rarely seem to take time for regular personal Bible study. Our Bible remains on the shelf, its message unexplored and unapplied. The result, however, of this shallow understanding of God's Word is *that we are not imprinted by the message of God's grace that lies at its core and is the beating heart of true Christianity.* We are Christians who have had a taste of God's goodness and love but we have not really grasped the wonder of God's grace.

Too many Christians live without a clear understanding of this message of grace and it can lead to some unintended consequences in our lives. The first consequence is that *we do not know the Christian message well enough to articulate it with clarity to others.* We find ourselves unable to defend Christianity against its many critics. We are unable to explain the good news of Jesus in simple language and therefore unable to lead others to Christ. Our shallow understanding of the Bible hinders our evangelism. In fact, without a clear grasp of the unique work of Jesus the need for us to engage in evangelism *at all* is brought into question. The second consequence is that *we fail to work out the implications of the cross in our own lives.* Some of us go through our Christian lives feeling condemned because of past sin; others go through our Christian lives pretending that sin is no longer a problem. We do not live day by day in the knowledge and experience of God's grace, which is the antidote for these wrong ways of thinking.

There is another problem that afflicts Christians (and this is a danger even for those who know the Bible well)—*the message of God's grace becomes displaced by something else.* Some of us by temperament enjoy the security that rules bring, and these rules can displace God's grace in our lives. We start to become judgmental of others and self-righteous in our Christianity because others are not keeping the rules in the way we are. Our Christianity then turns into impersonal religion (sometimes called *legalism*). Other Christians by temperament enjoy the comfort that pleasure brings. We start to find meaning and fulfilment in our pleasures rather than in God's grace. Our holidays, our TV programmes, our sport, our hobbies become the things we live for each day, rather than the Living God. Our Christianity then turns into unholy self-indulgence (sometimes called *lawlessness*).

If you recognise your life in any of the above descriptions this book is for you. It is about God's grace and why it is important in our lives. It is about the way that God shows unimaginable love to the undeserving. It is about the way that God has graciously intervened in history to deal once and for all time with the problem of our sin. It is about the grace of God that has been extended to each one of us at the cross of Jesus. In this book I want to help Christians to see that the gospel of God's grace is not just good news for people who want to become Christians, it is good news for those who are *already* Christians and are struggling with the daily reality of sin. The cross of Jesus is not just where we start in our Christian lives, it is the place we must come back to *day by day* to experience God's grace.

The priority of grace

In particular, this book is about the *priority* of grace. I maintain here that grace is of first importance for Christians. *First* because we are unable to make any response to God except that he first graciously opens our eyes and prompts us to respond by his Spirit. *First* because the message of God's grace in the cross is the core message and the defining feature of true Christianity. *First* because the message of God's grace in Jesus Christ is the only way that people can be rescued from sin and for him. *First* because grace is the first thing we must understand at the beginning of our Christian lives. *First* because God's grace is of utmost importance in sustaining us and shaping us as we continue throughout our Christian lives.

The premise of what follows is that a true understanding of God's grace in our lives will change everything. Once a person is gripped by the message of the cross, life can never be the same again. It will change our direction, our priorities and our passions. It will determine our eternal future.

This book is written primarily for those who have been Christians for a number of years but still only vaguely understand the Bible's teaching on grace. Those who want a fuller understanding of what Christ has done for them at the cross. Those who want to work out the implications of God's grace for their lives today. This book spells out the priority of grace in our Christian lives and how a firm understanding of the gospel can transform us. I dare to hope that this summary of the gospel and its implications will remind Christians of the joy that is ours in Christ, and that it will help us all to live for Christ with greater urgency and passion.

Finally, a word about how I have ordered the material in the book. There are three sections: *grace remembered, grace received and grace reapplied.* I want to demonstrate in these pages that Christians need daily reminders of God's grace to enable them to live for Christ. I want to suggest that we must actively and regularly pursue a deeper understanding of God's grace.

The first section is entitled *grace remembered.* Chapter 1 outlines the big story of God's grace found in the Bible. Chapter 2 then describes the events of the cross where God's grace was supremely displayed. This section will not only remind us of all that God has done for us in Jesus, but will also help us to articulate that message to others.

The second section is entitled *grace received.* Chapter 3

explores the power of the cross in our lives today as Christians. In chapter 4 we square up to the reality of our sinfulness as human beings before reminding ourselves in the following chapter of the hope that is ours because of God's grace. In this section we will see that God's grace needs to be received. We have an all-important response to make to God's grace in Jesus.

The final section is entitled *grace reapplied*. Here we recognise the need to continually reapply the message of God's grace in our lives. In doing so we are able to avoid the dangers of legalism and lawlessness that the Apostle Paul warns of in Philippians 3 (chapter 6) and reapply God's grace in our lives today (chapter 7).

Finally, in the conclusion I will draw these ideas together so that we can understand in practical terms what it means to live by grace day by day and why it should take priority in our Christian lives.

Section 1: Grace Remembered

I
What is it you believe again?

Exploring the 'big story' of God's grace

I once had a lively discussion with my dentist. Normally when I go to the dentist I do not get the opportunity to speak about my Christian beliefs because they fill my mouth with wads of cotton wool and instruments making any conversation tricky. I am also very aware that if the subject gets controversial, they've got a drill! However, on this particular day we got into conversation about God. I had never been seen by this dentist before, and she had noticed from my notes that I worked for a church (as I did then), and so her opening words as I walked into the surgery were something like: 'Well, you don't look as pious as I thought you'd look!' I wasn't sure whether that was a compliment or not, but I quickly realised that this was going to be an unusual visit to the dentist.

In fact, we had a long conversation about what it means to believe in God. At one point in the conversation I said something about the fact that God can rightfully demand our obedience if he is the one who has made us, and rules the universe. I could not see her face, but I remember that she reacted quite strongly. 'That is terrible,' she said, 'no-one should have to obey anyone else!'

That would be the view of many people in our society today, but the fact that God is our Creator is precisely where we need to start in understanding the Christian message. We need to understand that God rightly rules and owns everything. To understand the Christian message we need to go back to the very beginning of the Bible.

In this chapter I want to remind you of the 'big story' of the whole Bible. In doing so I want to emphasise again the overarching story of God's grace and its importance for our lives today, but also provide a framework for explaining the Christian message to others.

What's the story?

Another way of describing the Christian message is to talk about 'the gospel', by which we mean the joyful and life-changing message of 'God coming to the rescue by sending Jesus'. The gospel is wonderfully summarised by the words of John 3:16 (the most famous verse in the Bible): 'God so loved the world that he gave his one and only Son, that whoever believes in him shall not perish but have eternal life.'

It is this gospel story that is the main subject matter of the entire Bible, and its message unfolds progressively throughout its pages from Genesis to Revelation. We can summarise this story using four headings: Creation, Sin, Jesus and New Creation.

The lights go down and you settle into your seat with your popcorn in one hand and an oversized cup of drink in the other. Scenes from the newest box office release flash up in front of you and a deep male American voice intones through the speakers that surround you: 'It is the greatest love story ever told: the story of a man on a mission to rescue the world from danger, a story of personal sacrifice, a story of good overcoming evil, a story of new hope and second chances ...'

But this description is not Hollywood hype concerning its latest movie. This is a *true* story that involves everyone reading this book; in fact every person in the world, everyone who has ever lived. It has global, even eternal consequences. It is the story of how a loving God overcomes all the obstacles to win people back to himself. To understand this story, however, we need to rewind all the way back to Genesis 1.

The beginning: *Creation*

This story begins (as it ends) with God. The Bible opens with the words 'In the beginning *God* ...' (Genesis 1:1). World history and our own history begin with him. The Bible tells us that God is our Creator. He made the universe in all its beauty, wonder and complexity, and he made people (including you and me) in all our beauty, wonder and complexity. The evidence points to the fact that the Creator is good and powerful and involved with his world. He is not, as some seem to paint him today, some sort of distant and moody old man who has abandoned his world. He is loving and gracious. He is the one who keeps the planet spinning and the world he has made reflects his goodness and love in so many ways. He is not distant.

Recently my wife and I had the privilege of taking some African friends who live in a land-locked country to see the sea for the first time in their lives. I still remember them staring nervously at the waves with wide-eyed wonder. We then took them to a little aquarium to see the multi-coloured fish and sea creatures there. As we stood in a tunnel surrounded by the beauty and diversity of this marine world one of our friends turned to me and said with conviction 'How can people say there is no God?'

Just stand on a mountain top on a dark, starry night, or take a walk in the lush green countryside or go to the beach and watch the waves pounding the shore and you will see something of God's good handiwork. The Creator's fingerprints are all over his creation. Our world shouts a message that is thoroughly consistent with the message of the Bible, that God exists and that this good and powerful God is to be worshipped by all he has made.

In particular, human beings are viewed in Genesis 1 as being the very climax of God's creation: we are made 'in the image of God,' we've received God's blessing and are given a unique role in caring for God's world. We've been made to live in a close relationship with our Creator. This means that we must give him his rightful place in our lives; we must live in gratitude for his generous love and provision for us; we must recognise his right to rule over all of creation. God is the owner of our world, and *we* belong to him. There is no better way to live than submitting to God's authority.

When I insist that my three young children play in the garden and not on the busy road outside our house my restrictions are laid down out of concern for their good. Likewise, when God commands our obedience it is because he has good plans for our lives; he does not want us to come to harm. When a human being bows before their Creator it is not an abuse of our humanity, but is, in fact, the way to live life to the full.

People were never meant to live without God in their lives.

We were made to know God, to love him, and honour him. That is how it was for the first man and the first woman, Adam and Eve, in the very beginning. But a quick look around our world today, shows us that something has changed. We do not see the human race bowing the knee before their Creator and caring for the world he has made. If we are honest, many today don't give their Creator God a thought, except as a swear word. From experience we know that people often don't even care for each other, let alone God. There are lots of very selfish people in our world, including us, if the truth is told. The bottom line is that despite its ideal beginnings our world has changed for the worse.

The problem: *Sin*

You walk past the bakery and you see a cream cake that you can't resist; as you relate the story to someone else you say with a twinkle in your eye: 'I know I'm on a diet. I know it's *sinful* but I couldn't help it!' The word 'sin' is commonly used like that today. It is something that you do that's a bit naughty for some minor reason, but nice. However, the way many of us use the word 'sin' today is a million miles away from how it is used in the Bible. We need to realise that sin, as the Bible describes it (see chapter 4), is ugly and destructive. It eats away at the very foundations of what we have been made to be by God; it dehumanises us and it cuts the life cord between us and our loving Creator. It distorts the 'image of God' in us so that we no longer reflect God's character as we should.

This is the story of Genesis 3. It started with Adam and Eve in the paradise of the Garden of Eden. In a grubby attempt to be equal with God the first man and woman damaged their relationship with God and were expelled from his presence. The blessing of God upon humanity was replaced with God's curse because of this sin, and it has been humanity's greatest problem ever since. We have refused to give the Creator God his rightful place. From the very beginning, people have rejected God's way for their own way. We have tried to run our own lives without him. Like Adam and Eve we have tried to pull ourselves free of his grasp and live without acknowledging him. At best we have ignored God and at worst we have told him to 'get lost'! From the earliest moments of our lives we have joined this 'Get God out of our lives' campaign. And this harmful way of living has made our world dysfunctional. Nothing works properly anymore. It has badly affected all of our relationships. Now we catch only occasional glimpses of God's character in our own character and we have a tremendous potential for evil. Our desire is not to honour and serve the Creator, but rather to honour and serve ourselves. That is the world in which we live today.

In May 1981 a previously unknown disease was reported among drug-users and homosexuals in New York City, America. This life-threatening disease was found to be caused by a virus which broke down the body's natural defence to fight off infection and ultimately led to death. What is this killer disease? It is now known as Acquired Immune Deficiency Syndrome or AIDS. It was found to be caused by a destructive virus now called 'HIV' (Human Immunodeficiency Virus). Since 1981 this disease has spread and has marred the lives of millions of men, women and children across the globe. Yet, however deadly this awful disease may be, it is not as deadly as the disease that we are all infected by—sin. HIV can rob us of physical life but sin robs us of eternal life. Humanity is gripped by an incurable disease of selfishness that doctors will never be able to medicate. And, however much I might want to believe otherwise, the problem that plagues our world is not just out there somewhere, it actually lives in *me*. I have rebelled against God.

Our disregard for him rightly causes our Creator to be angry with us. Although created to be friends of God, we have made ourselves his enemies and chosen a path that leads to death. Because God cannot accept anything that is dark or impure he will not tolerate sin in our lives and will not allow it to continue unpunished. God's righteous punishment for sin, the Bible tells us, is death.[1] That is exactly what God promised Adam and Eve before they sinned.[2] The moment they first rebelled against God they became spiritually dead and separated from the Author of life, and in time they experienced physical death.

The same is true for us today the Bible says. Because of *our* sin we are dead already—spiritually dead[3]—and one day we will experience physical death. Whether we have committed big crimes in society, or simply ignored God we stand condemned on 'death row' because our sin has deadly consequences. Despite our best efforts we continue to be controlled by our sinful urges. We need to change somehow, but we are totally unable to help ourselves.

The Bible speaks about hell as a fearful reality for those who have rebelled against God. The Creator will hold those he has made accountable for their actions. There will be a day when every person who has ever lived will stand before him and justice will be done. In our better moments we long for that kind of justice. When we see evil in our world we want to see it punished. Murderers and rapists should pay for their crimes, we believe, but we don't use the same standard for the evil in our own lives. The truth is, however, that the darkness of our hearts, which hurts others and ultimately offends God, will be exposed and punished.

So is there any hope? Are we all condemned to death and to hell? Well, the Bible tells us that there *is* hope. It lies in the message of John 3:16: 'God so loved the world that he gave his one and only Son, that whoever believes in him shall not perish but have eternal life.' Just as Adam brought death to the living through his sin, so Jesus brings life to the dying through his perfect sacrifice. Enter God's hero—Jesus Christ.

The answer: *Jesus*

There is a fictional story told about the scientist Albert Einstein. Einstein was frequently asked to speak at various dinner functions, which he did not enjoy. He resented the time he had to spend away from his laboratory. One day as he was being driven to yet another of these dinners he explained to his chauffeur that he was tired of making speeches. As Einstein related this to the chauffeur, the man had an idea. He resembled Einstein in some ways and he had heard Einstein give his speech many times before. He felt confident that he could give the speech for him. So when they arrived at the dinner Einstein put on the chauffeur's cap and jacket and sat at the back of the room, and the chauffeur donned Einstein's clothes and sat at the top table. After dinner the chauffeur then gave an excellent version of Einstein's speech and was even able to expertly answer a few questions. But then he hit a problem. An extremely pompous professor stood up and asked a difficult question, making it clear to the audience that he knew exactly what he was talking about. The chauffeur was not deterred however. He looked at the professor and replied: 'Sir, the answer to your question is so simple that even my driver sitting at the back of the room will be able to answer it!'

This man had a brilliant response to an extremely difficult problem. God too, had a brilliant response to an extremely difficult problem. The problem was that human beings were messed up by sin and headed for disaster, but his life-changing response was to send his son—Jesus Christ—to the rescue. This is the story of grace in action that fills the pages of the Bible from Genesis 3 onwards. God treats rebellious people in a way that they don't deserve, and this amazing love of God is ultimately seen in God sending Jesus to deal with the problem of sin once and for all.

The story of human history is that we have offended and insulted the Living God with our lives, and that we are unable to help ourselves when it comes to sin. However, God in his goodness, quite literally stepped into our shoes to help. This is the wonderful story of God's grace to a rebellious world— God's Son came to live with us for a while to save us from our sin. And although he became human, just like us, although he knew all about the sort of pain and difficulty we experience in life, he never rebelled against his heavenly Father in the way we do. He never sinned. He was perfect in every way. In fact, he was the only person to ever live who has not messed up his life with sin. In fact, he has shown us what it means to be truly alive! However, Jesus was not just a good example (some people think of Jesus like that). He was the greatest rescuer this world has ever seen. It is true that Jesus ended up on a Roman cross, but it was no accident. It was God's plan (hinted at in the earliest pages of the Bible). The problem of sin was so severe that only Jesus' death in our place could bridge the gap between a rebellious humanity and the sinless Creator. Jesus chose to go to the cross so that he could deal with the curse of sin and death in our lives and remove the punishment of hell that hung over our heads. He took our punishment so that we could experience total forgiveness and a new start. Jesus died on a Roman cross with the weight of the world on his shoulders so that we could come back into right relationship with our Creator.

The ending: *New Creation*

I remember travelling once in a car with my mum and dad. I was a teenager at the time and therefore felt it was my right and duty to be somewhat embarrassed by my parents. We had just been to visit another family from our church who were struggling financially, and my parents were discussing in the front of the car how they could help. My dad kindly suggested that we could put some money in an envelope and post it through their front door with the words 'From the Lord Jesus Christ' written on the front. This I felt was a little pious, so I piped up from the back of the car: 'Wow! The postal system must be really bad; it took 2000 years to reach them!' Needless to say my comments were not appreciated.

Some people think in exactly that way. They think: 'What possible difference could Jesus' life and death have on my life today? Surely, I am about 2000 years too late to have a meaningful relationship with Jesus.' We must not think, however, that the cross was the end of Jesus. Make no mistake about the fact that Jesus is alive today. After three days Jesus defeated the grave. He is no longer dead and buried in a garden tomb outside the city of Jerusalem. He is risen! God raised him from the dead and declared him to be the King of everything. The crucified and risen Jesus has ascended to heaven to reign forever over God's kingdom. There he lives as God's champion. He is the one who has decisively defeated the powers of sin and death for us, and by the power of God's Spirit in our lives it is possible to know this great King and be in relationship with him.

But this is not quite the end of the story. The Bible tells us that the great King will be returning to our world[4] and when he does *everyone* will bow before him and recognise his right to reign as God's chosen King. When he does, justice will be done, and the wrongs of this world will be put right. When he does, every person who has ever lived (including you and me) will stand before the King of everything, and account for their lives. And on that day, the Bible tells us that Jesus, our Judge, will not be weighing our good deeds against our bad deeds to see whether we can experience eternal life. There will be many respectable, moral people who will not get to experience the life to come, because they rejected Jesus and his cross, because they refused to go to him for forgiveness. These people, along with all who have not acknowledged their Creator, will experience God's punishment of hell. But those who have turned to Jesus for forgiveness will be saved from their deserved punishment and experience the joy of eternal life.

The final scene of the Bible is of creation giving way to new creation, as our sinned-scared existence is transformed and God makes all things new. Then, we are told, heaven will come to earth and God will live with people forever. Then, death, mourning, crying and pain will all be history. The final chapters of the Bible use the language of the Garden of Eden to describe the paradise that we will enjoy as God's people. We are told that there will no longer be any curse from sin. There will be those from 'every tribe and language and people and nation' (Revelation 5:9) represented in God's new world. One day our world and its inhabitants will be at peace with their Creator once more.

You decide: One way or the other

This story then leaves us with the biggest decision of our lives. Will we choose grace or punishment? This decision even dwarfs the other life decisions we need to make such as whom to marry, what to study, what job to choose, where we will live. These are secondary to the decision we make about our Creator. Will we continue to rebel against the God of the Universe; a path that the Bible assures us leads to death? Or will we turn to him in desperation over our sin and experience his forgiveness; a path that the Bible assures us leads to eternal life? That is the fundamental decision that every human being needs to make.

John 3:36 makes a stark statement about this fundamental choice: 'Whoever believes in the Son has eternal life, but whoever rejects the Son will not see life, for God's wrath remains on him.' This is a life or death situation. The bad news is that we have all messed up and we are headed for disaster. The good news is that there is forgiveness and hope available in Jesus Christ—God's rescuer. That is the Christian message. That is the big story of God's grace.

The time has come

Mark tells us that Jesus started his ministry in Galilee with these words (Mark 1:15): 'The time has come … The kingdom of God is near. Repent and believe the good news.'

The response that Jesus commands of us in the light of his arrival as the conquering King is to 'repent and believe the good news'. The word 'repent' is cruelly lampooned by the media. Many see it as an archaic word with little relevance for a twenty-first century audience. However, the word literally means 'to change your mind'. So, what Jesus is calling for in the light of his arrival as King and Rescuer is 'a change of mind'. Actually, in biblical thought changing your mind is closely related to changing your behaviour. It is only as we get our thinking straightened out by God that we will get our lives straightened out by God. For example, the Apostle Paul writes in Romans 12:2 'Do not conform any longer to the pattern of this world, but be transformed by the renewing of your mind …'

In other words, transformed lives happen because of transformed minds. That is what Jesus is calling for in Mark 1:15—a radical change of mind that leads to a radical change of behaviour. Sometimes in the New Testament repentance is described as 'turning to God' (Acts 3:19). It is making a 180 degree turn. It requires us to turn from our old ways steeped in sin and turn to God so that we might walk in his ways. In the light of Jesus' coming he calls all people to make a U-turn.

Coupled with Jesus' command 'to repent' is his command 'to believe the good news' or as Paul describes it in Acts 20:21 to 'have faith in our Lord Jesus'.[5] We often speak about faith in a vague way nowadays. People say things like: 'I wish I had your faith' by which they seem to be saying that they are, for some reason, unable to summon up enough 'spirituality' (whatever that might be) to believe what you believe. Faith is also often seen as a personal possession: 'You have your faith, I have mine.' The implication seems to be that we are united by the idea of having a faith, but simply divided by what that faith is.[6] However, the Bible never refers to faith in these ways. Faith in the Bible always has an object. It is faith in someone or something. In Mark 1:15 Jesus calls people to put their faith *in* the good news of the kingdom.[7] In Acts 20:21 Paul states that he called people to faith *in* the Lord Jesus.

Life cannot continue as it has done before. The first coming of Jesus divides history into two. A radical response is required to God's offer of grace. We *must* repent and believe in Jesus.

The unrivalled King

We become quickly cynical nowadays about the claims of advertisers who insist that their product is the best and the only one worth buying. Whether it is bread or washing powder or a chocolate bar they extol their product's virtues above others. They insist that your life will be incomplete without it. Wear the right deodorant and it will improve your love life! Buy the right bathroom cleaner and the bathroom will clean itself! The problem is that (personal preference aside) we know that one bathroom cleaner is much the same as any other. There are many products on offer and the benefits of one over the other are actually slight.

We must not, however, make that mistake with Jesus. The Bible is not making an advertiser's claim about Jesus being 'the best' and 'the only' when in reality we know that there are many other kings and rescuers on offer and the benefits of following Jesus are only slight. This is not just commercial rhetoric to get the Christian 'product' noticed above the others. The Bible insists that, although there are many pretenders, Jesus is the *real* King. He makes unique claims. He does not claim to be one way among many to reach God (as is the spirit of the age). He claims that he is the universal King who calls the people of the world to experience true life and forgiveness through him. Such a view may well be considered to be the height of intolerance nowadays but the witness of the Bible is not easily brushed aside.

In Matthew 28:18 the risen Jesus says that 'All authority in heaven and on earth has been given to me ...' In other words, he is the unrivalled King who will have the final victory. And it is *this* great King who has declared that a relationship with God is only possible through him. He says 'I am the way and the truth and the life. No-one comes to the Father except through me.' (John 14:6) This seems to comprehensively rule out any other trailblazer or 'truth' teller or 'life' giver except Jesus. The apostles, who were eye witnesses of his life, death and resurrection, announced the same message. Peter, for example, states 'Salvation is found in no-one else, for there is no other name under heaven given to people by which we must be saved.' (Acts 4:12) Again, it is clear that an exclusive claim is being made—that Jesus is the *only* one who can save people from their sin. The problem of sin is not going to be dealt with by anyone or anything else. Notice also the urgency of Peter's statement. He does not say 'by which we can be saved'. He says 'by which we *must* be saved'. Being saved by Jesus is not a lifestyle option. It is a divine command. As the Apostle Paul says the coming of Jesus means that: '[God] commands all people everywhere to repent' (Acts 17:30). There is no way of excusing ourselves from the obvious realisation that this must include you and me.

Endnotes

1   Romans 6:23
2   Genesis 2:17
3   Ephesians 2:1
4   Revelation 22:20
5   The Greek word translated as 'believe' is *pisteuete* and in Acts 20:21 'faith' is *pistin*. One is a verb, the other a noun but they have the same root meaning.

6 It also seems to be implied that it would be rude for me to recommend *my faith* to you.
7 The good news of the kingdom is that God's liberating king has come, so there is an implicit call to faith *in* Jesus in Mark 1:15 too.

2
The crux of the matter

Understanding the cross

Before I became a pastor and a Bible college lecturer I studied Chemistry, and part of my course required me to work on a project over a number of months, which I then wrote up and handed in to my supervisor. I worked hard at my project; I wanted it to be really good. So I was extremely shocked when I discussed my work with my supervisor and he accused me of being lazy and of cheating. I still remember the pain of that moment. I was really indignant and upset at the injustice. I knew that I had worked hard, and that I had been wrongly accused.

Now try to imagine that feeling of injustice and then magnify it by a million! In doing so, you will begin to understand something of the injustice of Jesus' trial and execution. What happened to Jesus was outrageously undeserved and unjust, and yet the amazing truth is that God was at work in the events of the cross in a way that no-one imagined.

In 1 Corinthians 2:2 the Apostle Paul writes about the importance of the cross in his Christian life. He states '… I resolved to know nothing while I was with you except Jesus Christ and him crucified.' We need to have the same commitment as Christians. The cross of Jesus should fill our vision and shape our lives. In this chapter we literally come to the crux of the gospel. The word 'crux' is a Latin word that means 'cross' but we use it in English nowadays to talk about the most important thing in a certain discussion. Well, the most important thing in Christianity is the message of the cross. This is the crux of the matter. Jesus' achievements at the cross are the heart of our faith and the supreme demonstration of the grace of God.

The title of this book was inspired by Paul's words in 1 Corinthians 15:3 'For what I received I passed on to you *as of first importance*: that Christ died for our sins according to the Scriptures …' There can be no more important subject for the Christian than this. However, we need to be sure that our thinking about the cross is not based on uninformed speculation or popular notions but rather on reliable eye-witness evidence.[1] That is why we need to turn to the Bible and in this case to the account that Luke gives us in Luke 23 of that day that changed history forever.

What happened at the cross?

Let's think about the events that led up to the cross. Jesus is arrested in the darkness of Thursday night in the Garden of Gethsemane. He is brought before both Annas and Caiaphas[2] overnight, where he is mocked and beaten. At daybreak on Friday morning the Jewish Ruling Council[3] meet and they decide that Jesus should die for blasphemy. However, the

Council had no legal power to execute anyone; they needed the help of the Romans to do that. So Jesus is brought before Pilate—the Roman Governor of Judea—who declares Jesus to be innocent, but who in turn, sends him to Herod—who ruled over Galilee for the Romans.4 Herod questions Jesus, but Jesus remains silent. Again he is mocked and insulted, this time by Herod and his soldiers. Jesus is then returned to Pilate, who stills believes Jesus to be innocent, but does not have the courage to stand up to the crowd who are calling for his blood. Finally, Barabbas, a revolutionary and murderer, is released from prison to walk the streets of Jerusalem as a free man, but Jesus, who is innocent of any charges, is sent to his death. The Jewish religious leaders have not only been unjust in condemning an innocent man, they have also plotted together to murder their own Christ5 and in doing so they have rejected God himself. It is these two themes of Jesus' innocence and Jesus being God's chosen King that run throughout Luke 23.

Jesus is God's chosen King

A number of years ago I took the train every week from Lowestoft (where I was living at the time) to London. As I arrived at London Liverpool Street I never once had the following experience: I never arrived to the sound of a brass band playing the national anthem, nor did I ever find a red carpet stretching down the concourse, nor were there ever great crowds of people waving Union flags and shouting 'God save the king!' Actually, what happened every week was that I got off the train, nobody even noticed my arrival in the Capital and I quickly got lost in a swell of people making their way to the Tube station. Now, of course, there is a very good reason for me not to receive a royal reception—I am not the king of England! There is no royal blood running through my veins. Nobody would ever mistake me for royalty as I enter the Capital. However, on Palm Sunday, just a few short days before the events of the cross Jesus was given just such a royal reception as he entered Jerusalem (Luke 19:28ff.) There were many excited disciples who had understood Jesus' teaching that he was God's chosen King—the Christ. They had witnessed his miracles and they believed that now Jesus was coming to Jerusalem to take his throne, and so they enthusiastically welcome Jesus as the new king of Israel.

They say that a week is a long time in politics, and certainly a few days made a great difference for Jesus. In that time public opinion in Jerusalem radically changed. It is now Thursday evening and four chapters later (Luke 23). Jesus is on his own; even his closest disciples have run for their lives. He is standing before religious and secular authorities who are deciding whether he should live or die. Luke 23 is full of references to Jesus being God's King, but here it is an idea that few seem to be taking seriously.

In v.11 the idea of Jesus being a king becomes a cruel joke between King Herod and Pilate. Herod and his soldiers dress Jesus in an 'elegant robe'. They ridicule him. Who does he think he is pretending he's a king? Herod shares his cruel joke with Pilate. He sends his prisoner back to him dressed like a king! It seems that the idea of Jesus' kingship was everyone's joke that day.

Later when Jesus hung on the cross (v.35), the religious leaders challenged him to prove he really was God's King. The Roman soldiers joined in too (v.36): 'If you are the king of the Jews, save yourself'. Even the sarcastic charge against Jesus that hung above his head on the cross was: 'This is the king of the Jews.' (v.38) Luke, the Gospel writer, wants you to notice the irony. This prisoner hanging on a cross between two criminals is actually God's chosen King. He is the Christ.

Jesus is innocent of any charges

There is, however, another theme that runs throughout this chapter that Luke wants us to notice. He wants his readers to understand that Jesus is totally innocent. Even the human courts that tried Jesus found him to be innocent. Notice that Pilate states (v.4) that he has found 'no basis for a charge against this man.' When Jesus is returned to Pilate from Herod (v.14) Pilate tells Jesus' Jewish accusers:

> 'You brought me this man as one who was inciting the people to rebellion. I have examined him in your presence and have found no basis for your charges against him. Neither has Herod, for he sent him back to us; as you can see he has done nothing to deserve death.'

Again, after the crowd calls for Jesus' crucifixion, Pilate replies (v.22): 'Why? What crime has this man committed? I have found no grounds for the death penalty.' Later, (v.41) as Jesus hangs on the cross one of the criminals who hung there with him said the same: 'We are punished justly, for we are getting what our deeds deserve. But this man has done nothing wrong.' Luke wants you to notice the injustice. This prisoner hanging on a cross between two criminals is totally innocent of any crime.

As we examine Luke 23:32–43 we find recorded the last minutes of Jesus' life. And, to be honest, for Christians this is a story that causes mixed emotions. It is difficult to know whether to laugh with joy or cry with sadness. We rejoice in the victory of the cross, and yet we mourn the agony and sinfulness of this moment. The cross is both a moment of triumph and of tragedy.

Jesus forgives his enemies (vv.32–34)

This has been a gruelling night for Jesus. He has been dragged back and forth between various authorities where he has been repeatedly questioned. He has been mocked. He has been spat on, and struck on the head with a staff many times. He has been flogged. Jesus is now in a weakened state. So much so that the Roman soldiers force a man from the crowd to carry Jesus' cross for him. Normally the condemned person would have carried their own cross to the place of execution.

Luke wants us to notice the tremendous irony of this innocent king being executed among common criminals at a place called 'the Skull'. Look at the way he describes the event (v.32):

'Two other men, both criminals, were also led out to be executed. When they came to the place called the Skull, there they crucified him, along with the criminals—one on his right, the other on his left.'

However, it is not just the irony of the event that Luke wants us to see. He also wants us to recognise that even this dark moment of history was part of God's plan. He points out for us that Jesus' crucifixion fulfilled Old Testament prophecy. Back in Luke 22:37 Jesus applies the words of Isaiah 53:12 to himself '... he was numbered with the transgressors.' And that is exactly what Luke is drawing our attention to here—Jesus is being executed *'with the transgressors'*. He hangs between two criminals.

Notice Jesus' startling words as the soldiers hang him on the cross; as they divide up his last earthly possessions and shout their insults (v.34): 'Father, forgive them, for they do not know what they are doing.' In the middle of the pain, the sarcasm and the angry insults Jesus prays for the forgiveness of his executioners! Those who nailed him to that cross did not realise the full extent of their crimes; they were killing the author of life, but as they crucify him Jesus, with unimaginable compassion, prays *for their forgiveness*!

Jesus' example here makes our own lives look grubby in comparison. We can be very slow, as Christians, to forgive others. We can simply refuse to move on from hurtful words and actions. Some of us would rather move churches than be reconciled to other Christians in the congregation. I am not suggesting that it is easy, but sometimes our disputes are petty in the light of God's coming Kingdom, and we must seek God's help to forgive others. Sometimes our lack of forgiveness speaks more of own wounded pride and loss of self-image than of the severity of others' sins against us. Of course, this is not always the case. At the other extreme, there are times when the sin that has been committed against us is truly horrific and leaves us with deep emotional scars for the rest of our lives. However, whether the crimes against us are big or small they do not compare to the sin of the cross. The words of Jesus from the cross *'Father, forgive ...'* stand in stark contrast too often to our own words and attitudes as God's people.

Jesus chooses not to save himself, but others (vv.35–43)
When I started secondary school, our class was taken to the

local pool for swimming lessons. It was during these school lessons that I was awarded a medal for my swimming. In theory this is something I should have been proud of, but in reality I was not for two reasons. First, it was a bronze medal—I never reached the heady heights of silver or gold. And secondly, it was a medal for 'personal survival'! I cannot help but smile every time I think about my swimming medal. It all seems a little perverse. Imagine that I am swimming around in the sea one day when I come across someone struggling to stay afloat and shouting for help. In that situation my bronze medal is no help whatsoever. Am I meant to shout to the drowning person 'Sorry, I'm not qualified to rescue you … I only have a medal for personal survival' and then swim off to safety? Surely, it is people who risk their lives for others who deserve medals, not those who are interested in personal survival!

Luke makes it quite clear here that Jesus—God's chosen King—was more interested in saving others, than he was in personal survival. He tells us that there were four groups of people who witnessed Jesus' death. First, there was a crowd of people who merely watched as Jesus died (v.35). They were simply spectators who looked on from a distance. It seems that they did nothing to hurt Jesus, but they did nothing to help him either. If they had believed that Jesus really was God's King, they might have rushed to his aid, but they did not. We know that even some of Jesus' own disciples were there, but they didn't sacrifice their lives in a courageous attempt to help Jesus. Then we are told about another group of people (v.35). Luke tells us that the rulers—the Jewish religious leaders—*'sneered at him'*. They gloated over Jesus' misfortune. They were enjoying this moment. It is obvious from their words that they did not believe that he was God's King either. They shouted sarcastically 'He saved others let him save himself if he is the Christ of God, the Chosen One.' The third group (v.36) were the soldiers who also mocked Jesus' claim to kingship: 'If you are the King of the Jews, save yourself.' The last group who witnessed Jesus' death were the two dying criminals who were executed alongside Jesus (vv.39–43). Even one of these dying men used his last minutes of life to question Jesus' kingship 'Aren't you the Christ? Save yourself and us!'

'*Save yourself!*' That was their sarcastic message. If you really are who you claim to be, save yourself! You managed to do miracles for the benefit of others; you healed the sick; now save yourself! Many of the onlookers revelled in Jesus' apparent lack of power; they rejoiced in his weakness. Despite his claims to be a king, he did not seem to have much authority at this moment. His subjects were not rushing to his aid. His kingdom looked extremely small and insignificant on that day. No-one really believed those words that hung over Jesus' head. He was very much alone. He was everyone's joke. The crowd watched without doing anything. The rulers, his Roman executioners, and even one of the dying men on a nearby cross were all taking the opportunity to 'kick him whilst he was down'. This Jesus, it seemed, was not very good at self-preservation. He had come to a bloody and violent end on a Roman cross.

'*Save yourself!*' was their cry, but what his gloating enemies could never have imagined was that Jesus was not there to save himself. Just hours before this in the Garden of Gethsemane he had wrestled in prayer (Luke 22:42): 'Father, if you are willing, take this cup from me; yet not my will, but yours be done.' This humiliating event was not about personal survival. He hung on that cross to save others. This innocent King was dying for his guilty subjects; the righteous for the unrighteous;

the good for the bad. This event was to change a sinful world forever. It was him *for us*, that day. This moment of apparent weakness, was actually a moment of costly victory. The greatest of all kings stooped to conquer. He laid aside his majesty to rescue a lost world, amid jeers and pain. If you are a Christian you need to realise again that it is *by his wounds* that you have been healed (1 Peter 2:24).

I love the way that Jesus forgives and reassures the dying criminal who puts his faith in him in his last hours of life. What an incredible act of mercy! Unlike the other criminal who used his last energy to poke fun at Jesus, this man recognised that Jesus *was* who he claimed to be. This dying man had an insight into the situation that seemed to elude everyone else. He could see what no-one else could see. He recognised the King on the cross. 'Don't you fear God?' he asked the other criminal as they both stared death in face. Clearly the criminal asking the question *did* fear God; he recognised that he would have to answer to God for a badly lived life. He knew that they were both guilty. Their punishment had been justly given, but Jesus was innocent.

I can only guess that this man had come across Jesus before. He was, after all, a well-known figure. Maybe he knew Jesus' claims. Maybe he had heard Jesus teaching the crowds. Maybe he had been on trial at the same time as Jesus and had had a grandstand view of Jesus' defence. Whatever his previous contact with Jesus was, his request to Jesus as they both hung on the cross displays an incredible understanding of Jesus' divine kingship. He cries 'Jesus, remember me when you come into your kingdom.'

This man recognised that he was helpless to save himself, but incredibly he recognised power to save in the man dying

next to him! He believed that *Jesus* could save him. Maybe he
did not know much, but he knew that Jesus was his only hope.
He was dying; he only had minutes, at most hours, to live! All
he could do was plead with Jesus for mercy. 'Remember me!'
he cried to Jesus. And Jesus remarkably told this dying man
(v.43) 'I tell you the truth, today you will be with me in paradise.'

Notice that Jesus does not tell him that he would love to be
able to forgive him, but actually he needed to do some Old
Testament Bible study first to fully understand his claims. He
does not regretfully inform him that he needed to be baptised
first before he could enter the kingdom of God. He does not
tell him that his life had been too bad, that he had neglected
his religious duties or that only morally good people are saved
by God. Instead, he said words that must have filled this man
with hope as his life faded away. Jesus told him that he would
enjoy paradise *with him* and it would happen on that very day.
Simple faith in Jesus was enough to secure him a glorious
future. In that moment, this man's future was changed forever
as Jesus freely gave him eternal life. Instantly, his hopeless
situation was replaced with the hope of being with Jesus in
paradise. This forgiven criminal would find his way back into
Eden, back into God's presence, because of the man dying in
agony on the cross nearby.

Why did Jesus die?

I wonder if you can remember your most embarrassing moment.
I remember speaking to a student once who told me her most
embarrassing moment to date. She was at home and came into
a room to see her father with his back to her mending their
TV. They were obviously a close family because she decided
to play a trick on her dad. She crept up behind him, and before

he realised she was there, she pushed her cold hands up his tee-shirt onto his warm back. It was only at that moment that she realised that the man whom she had thought was her father was actually the TV repair man! At that moment, there were two very surprised people in the room. This girl had totally misread her situation; she had made a big mistake; a mistake that turned out to be extremely embarrassing.

Some people think the same is true of Jesus. They tell us that the cross was a big mistake. Jesus misread his situation. He didn't realise that the Jewish leaders would conspire against him; he under-estimated their jealousy. And in the end he was overtaken by his circumstances. He was a good man in the wrong place at the wrong time. Some even suggest that Jesus' final words on the cross prove this idea because he says '*It is finished!*' (John 19:30). They understand Jesus to be saying something like 'I'm finished!' or 'It's over!' But was Jesus really taken by surprise by the events leading up to the cross? Does that fit the biblical evidence? Was it all just a terrible mistake? Well, any sensible reading of the Gospels will not allow us to entertain that idea. The Bible tells us that the life of Jesus, even the sad and sinful events that led to the cross, happened according to God's plan. God was sovereignly at work bringing good out of evil. This was no accident—God was in control. That final cry from the cross '*It is finished!*' was not a cry of despair but a cry of victory—Jesus the Christ had completed his Father's rescue mission.

God's plan to rescue people from their sin was accomplished through the blood-soaked man on the cross. This is where the Bible had been pointing from the earliest chapters of Genesis. We are not taking the Bible seriously if we maintain that Jesus' death was just a freak accident. In Luke's Gospel alone the plan of God is clearly seen in Jesus' foreknowledge about the cross. Luke tells us that Jesus predicted his death on three separate occasions long before it happened.[6] First in Luke 9:22, then Luke 9:44 and finally in Luke 18:31–33:

> 'Jesus took the Twelve aside and told them, 'We are going up to Jerusalem, and everything that is written by the prophets about the Son of Man will be fulfilled. He will be turned over to the Gentiles. They will mock him, insult him, spit on him, flog him and kill him. On the third day he will rise again.''

Jesus' words here also show that he understood his suffering and death as a fulfilment of words written hundreds of years before by the prophets in the Old Testament (e.g. Isaiah 52:13–53:12). His death was not a tragic accident; it was the plan of God revealed to the prophets and soon to be fulfilled in Jerusalem. Jesus was not overwhelmed by his personal circumstances. It was the path he chose to walk. He went to the cross motivated by a divine love for human beings—even rebellious ones.[7] There was no other way. Jesus knew that death awaited him in Jerusalem. In fact, his death on the cross was the climax of his earthly ministry. He did not die as a martyr for a dying cause; he died as the greatest of all rescuers to bring eternal life. In Acts 2:23 we are told that Jesus: 'was handed over [to death] by God's set purpose and foreknowledge'. It is true that his death was the vicious and evil plan of jealous men,[8] but mysteriously and more fundamentally it was the gracious plan of God from before the creation of the world.[9]

But what difference does the cross make to us two thousand years later? In what ways does the cross have a powerful life-changing effect today? To this we now turn.

Endnotes

1   Luke 1:1–4
2   Caiaphas was the High Priest at the time. His father-in-law, Annas, had been the previous High Priest and still had tremendous influence.
3   Sometimes called 'the Sanhedrin'.
4   Jesus came from Galilee (Matthew 2:22–23).
5   Or Messiah. It literally means 'the anointed one'. Throughout the Old Testament God had promised to send a King who would perfectly reign over his people in a way that all the kings of Israel had failed to do. First century Jews lived with the hope that God would send them 'the Christ'.
6   The fact that Jesus knew he was soon to die is also clear from the final Passover meal he shared with his disciples (Luke 22:19–20) and his prayer in the Garden of Gethsemane (Luke 22:42).
7   1 John 4:9–10
8   John 11:47–53
9   Ephesians 1:4

Section 2: Grace Received

3
The power of the cross

What has Jesus' sacrifice achieved for us?

I remember as a child playing with my brother on a haystack on my grandparent's small farm. We loved going to the farm because there were so many great places for young boys to play—many of them, as I look back now with the eyes of a parent, incredibly dangerous! On this particular day we decided to play a game, which probably involved some sort of fighting, on top of a haystack. The stack was beside an overgrown area of land, which contained a large patch of stinging nettles that would have towered over any adult, let alone a child. Well, the inevitable happened. We will quickly skip over the subject of 'did he fall or was he pushed', and move to the part of the story where I had fallen off the haystack and into a jungle of stinging nettles, and I could not get out. As I didn't know what to do, I did what any other self-respecting child would have done in the same situation—I cried! My brother meanwhile went off to get help, and help came in the person of my dad. And on his arrival he did for me what I could not do for myself. He made a path through the stinging nettles to get me out, and he carried me inside the house so that I could get copious amounts of cream for the many stings that I had received in my fall.

This story is inadequate at many levels as an illustration of what Christ has done for us on the cross, but it does show us something. When Jesus died on the cross he became our rescuer; he graciously provided *a way out* for people who were trapped by the age-old problem of sin and death. To be honest, I don't think it cost my dad much to rescue me; he probably got a few stings, but it cost Jesus everything on the cross to rescue us. He experienced separation from his Father on the cross because of our sin.[1] He quite literally suffered hell on the cross in our place! He was abandoned and forsaken so that we need never be.

This chapter is simply an introduction to the subject of what Christ has achieved on the cross for us. Others have written entire books on this awe-inspiring subject.[2] However, even as we scratch the surface in our understanding of the achievements of the cross, let's see the wonderful difference that God's grace makes to our lives today.

We are free

The Bible tells us that Jesus' cross has set us free. To understand the wonder of God's rescue through the cross we must first recognise that human experience *without the cross* is a death trap. Paul writes about life without Christ (Titus 3:3)

'At one time we too were foolish, disobedient, deceived and enslaved by all kinds of passions and pleasures. We lived in malice and envy, being hated and hating one another ...'

In particular, the Bible pictures people as being enslaved to sin and the fear of death, and being captive to the devil as the one who holds the power of death.[3] However, the cross has set us free from these things that have such a hold over us and enslave us.

When we first arrived in Africa we lived in the mountainous country of Lesotho. For our first months there we lived in two rooms of a village house with no electricity and no running water. This was quite a challenge for us for a number of reasons. Benjamin, our son, was only eight months at the time and we were new to parenting, let alone parenting in such basic conditions as these. Much of my time was spent collecting, boiling and filtering water that dripped from a nearby tap just so we had enough water to drink and wash in. The title of one of our early prayer letters read 'Worms in the water, bats in the bedroom and ants in our pants!' The latter referring to the time when termites ate through the wall of the house and ate my wife's underwear! There were days in our first few months in Lesotho when we felt under attack.

In a more fundamental way all human beings are under attack. The Bible tells us that the powers of evil are real and that Satan is a real enemy who seeks to enslave us and destroy us, but it also tells us that Jesus has set us free through the cross. Paul writes of Christ's victory over evil in Colossians 2:15: '... having disarmed the powers and authorities, he made a public spectacle of them, triumphing over them by the cross.' Jesus states in John 8:36 regarding our slavery to sin '... if the Son sets you free, you will be free indeed.'

It is time to recognise the life-changing power of the cross—those who put their faith in the King on the cross have been rescued and we are free!

We are forgiven

The Bible tells us that Jesus' cross has brought us forgiveness of sins. The Apostle Paul asserts that 'There is no-one righteous, not even one' (Romans 3:10) and that 'all have sinned and fall short of the glory of God' (Romans 3:23). As we saw in chapter 1 our rebellion against God has earned us death, spiritual death and eventually physical death, just as it did for Adam and Eve when they first sinned. Yet the life-transforming message of the gospel is that: '... God demonstrates his own love for us in this: While we were still sinners, Christ died for us' (Romans 5:8). Christ did not die for morally good people, he died for bad ones; he died in our place when we were 'still sinners'. And for the Christian the wonderful truth is that Christ has forgiven *every* sin on the cross[4]—there are none that remain unforgiven! Only on this side of the cross can we feel the real impact of Psalm 103:12 that God's love for his people is so great that 'as far as the east is from the west so far has he removed our transgressions from us.'

According to the New Testament our forgiveness through the cross has two important consequences:

a. We are now no longer guilty in God's sight

The Bible tells us that we are now no longer guilty in God's sight because of the cross. One of the verses I repeatedly come back to as I realise again the depth of my own sin is Romans 8:1 where Paul writes that '... there is now *no condemnation* for those who are in Christ Jesus ...' Here is the objective reality. I may *feel* condemned for my sin but I am not. If I am a Christian (if I am 'in Christ Jesus' as Paul puts it here) then I will no longer face the deserved punishment of God for my sin. Of course, that was not always the case (notice the 'now');

something has happened in time and space to make this true for God's people, that God no longer counts our sin against us.⁵ That something is the work of the cross.

Another word the New Testament uses to describe this idea is 'justification'. It is a legal declaration of righteousness in God's sight because of the cross. In other words, God looks at us and sees the righteousness of his Son. Paul writes in Romans 1:17 '… in the gospel a righteousness from God is revealed, a righteousness that is by faith from first to last …' By faith in Jesus we have been given a 'righteousness from God' to replace the righteousness of our best deeds, which constantly prove to be insufficient to meet God's perfect standards.

We have noticed that the electrical items we have bought since coming to Africa have not lasted very long. We seem to have got through more than our fair share of kettles, toasters, DVD players and phones in the space of just a few years. Sometimes this has happened because our electrical goods have been 'fried' because of a lightning strike or a power surge, but often it is simply because they were faulty in some way. However, it is a wonderful thing when your appliances are still within their warranty period and you can take them back to the shop for a replacement. Your faulty furred up kettle, for example, can be exchanged for a shiny new one with a brand new element. Well, the same dynamic is at work at the cross—faulty lives get exchanged for new ones. The righteousness of Jesus replaces the broken deeds of our lives. Of course, this is where my illustration breaks down (forgive the pun) because if it is to mirror God's grace then the replacement kettle would be a perfect one that would last forever! This is something that electrical goods manufacturers are unlikely to achieve, but this is exactly what God achieves in our lives because of the cross.

We are changed forever. In God's court we are no longer guilty. There is no longer a stain on our character. We are clean. There is no condemnation. We have been declared 'righteous' because Christ's righteousness has been given to us.

It is time to recognise the life-changing power of the cross—those who put their faith in the King on the cross are now *no longer guilty in his sight.*

b. God is now no longer angry with us

The Bible tells us that God is now no longer angry with us because of the cross. The Apostle Paul describes our pre-Christian life in Ephesians 2:3: 'All of us ... lived ... at one time gratifying the cravings of our sinful nature and following its desires and thoughts. Like the rest, we were by nature objects of wrath.'

In other words God was rightly angry with us because of our sin. The very fact that our sin arouses God's righteous anger demonstrates the seriousness of sin. It is a curse upon each of us; we are '*by nature* objects of [God's] wrath.' However, what we are naturally has been overcome by a supernatural work of God at the cross, which has changed this situation forever for the believer. God's righteous anger, which was once directed at us, was there directed at his Son. God has been placated at the cross once and for all time and this has happened because he has *placated himself.* He is now no longer angry with those who put their faith in Jesus. The biblical word for the idea of 'removing God's anger' is propitiation. We are told in 1 John 4:10, for example, that Jesus is the one who removes God's anger: 'In this is love, not that we have loved God but that he loved us and sent his Son to be the propitiation for our sins.'[6]

It is time to recognise the life-changing power of the cross—
God is now no longer angry with those who put their faith in
the King on the cross.

We are reconciled to God

The Bible tells us that Jesus' cross has reconciled us to God.
We live in a world of dysfunctional relationships. We are no
strangers to estrangement. 'Divorce,' 'separation,' 'conflict'
and 'hostility' are words commonly found in our newspapers.
However, the Bible tells us that it is not just our human
relationships that are broken—our relationship with God is
too. This hostile relationship between people and God is the
consequence of personal sin. In fact, the Bible speaks about
us being enemies of God. Paul writes in Colossians 1:21 'Once
you were alienated from God and were enemies in your minds
because of your evil behaviour.'

However, through the cross Christians have been reconciled
to God. Reconciliation is the literal meaning of the theological
word 'atonement' ('at-one-ment'). The word 'reconciliation'
is only found in a few places in the New Testament but it is
an important theme nevertheless. It speaks of the new relationship
with God that is formed once the problem of sin has been dealt
with.[7] The war is over; we are now at peace with God.

The Apostle Paul states in Romans 5:1: '... since we have been
justified through faith, we have peace with God through our
Lord Jesus Christ ...' This peace with God has been achieved
through the cross (Colossians 1:22): '... now [God] has reconciled
you by Christ's physical body through death to present you holy
in his sight, without blemish and free from accusation ...'

Paul makes it clear that we can claim no part in God's gracious
initiative to renew sinful, hostile human beings and to reconcile

them to himself (2 Corinthians 5:18); 'All this is from God, who reconciled us to himself through Christ …'

One of the things I enjoy most about working at Namibia Evangelical Theological Seminary (NETS) is the diversity of our staff and students. We currently have staff from America, Australia, Germany, the Netherlands, the United Kingdom, Zambia and Zimbabwe. Our students are from a number of countries in southern Africa and most of the tribal and racial groups of Namibia are represented in our student body. In addition, our staff and students are from many different denominations. We are incredibly diverse in our backgrounds but we are united by the gospel of God's grace. From a human perspective our unity is astounding, but that 'horizontal' reconciliation has been achieved through the work of the cross. It is a tangible sign that God is at work among us and it reassures us that Christ has achieved a 'vertical' reconciliation for us too. The intimacy of the Garden of Eden has been restored through the cross. We can now be friends with one another and friends of God; the war is over through the greatest of peacemakers.

It is time to recognise the life-changing power of the cross— those who put their faith in the King on the cross are *reconciled to God*.

We have eternal life

We often don't like to think about it, but the truth is that we are all in the process of dying! Whether we are young or old, in good health or poor, beautiful or plain, rich or poor, famous or unknown we are all walking along a road that leads ultimately to death. It is just a matter of time. Death provides us with the ultimate statistic: one in one people die. That means (unless

Jesus returns beforehand) that one day those we love will attend
our funerals and stand around our graves. Death is a fact of
life. It is, of course, an unmentionable fact to pass comment
on in polite conversation, but it is a fact nevertheless. We can
ignore death; we can laugh at it; we can dismiss it as unimportant,
but left to our own devices one thing we cannot do is escape
its clutches. The Bible tells us that there is only one who can
save us from death's icy grip; the one whose grave is empty
because he rose again. Jesus Christ took our death penalty on
the cross and defeated death three days later and in doing so
he has brought hope beyond the grave—eternal life—to those
who put their trust in him. The New Testament says that
believers have moved from death to life. We were once dead
in our sins, but now we have been made alive through the
saving power of the cross and the empty grave. Paul writes in
Ephesians 2:4–5: '... because of his great love for us, God,
who is rich in mercy, made us alive with Christ even when we
were dead in transgressions—it is by grace you have been saved!'

The Bible tells us that Jesus' cross and empty grave bring
eternal life to those who put their faith in him. Life in Christ
is not simply the promise of a better life in the 'here and now',
but is also a promise of fullness of life in eternity. Jesus declared
(John 11:25–26): 'I am the resurrection and the life. He who
believes in me will live, even though he dies; and whoever lives
and believes in me will never die.'

Just as sin led to spiritual and physical death for all from
Adam's race[8] so through Jesus, the 'man from heaven,' we receive
new spiritual life and the promise of new physical life. The
grave will not be the end for those who are trusting in the one
who has decisively defeated the grave. Our physical bodies will
decay and die, but believers will live on 'with Christ' in heaven[9]

until the day when we will receive new 'resurrection bodies'.[10] Even now we experience the reality of eternal life through being in a joyful and fulfilling relationship with the Living God,[11] but there is so much more to come. One day we will be with Christ for eternity.

It is time to recognise the life-changing power of the cross and the empty grave—those who put their faith in the King on the cross will experience *eternal life*.

We are now the children of God

Several years ago I attempted to update my UK driving licence, but found that the authorities would not process my application because there was a question over my identity. In my old driving licence my name was misspelt. It had one extra letter. To be honest, I had noticed the mistake years ago but didn't think it warranted going through the rigmarole of getting my name corrected. This extra letter, however, turned out to be a bigger problem that I had expected because during the security checks it was noticed that my name was spelt differently on my driving licence to that on my passport and my birth certificate. This was enough to stop my application for a new driving licence until I could prove my identity. In the end a friend who has known me for twenty years had to sign the back of my photograph stating that this was my true identity.

It is fundamentally important for us as Christians to recognise our true identity. Jesus is clear about the fact that we are now no longer slaves to sin, but permanent members of God's family.[12] It would be easy to view ourselves simply as miserable sinners who have narrowly escaped God's punishment of death (for that is what we are!) However, we must recognise the new status attributed to those who have been rescued at the cross—

we are part of the family now. The New Testament thrills us with the thought that we have been adopted into God's family. We are now the children of God. In a way we could never have believed possible before we now belong to God. John writes in the introduction to his Gospel (John 1:12–13):

> '... to all who received him [Jesus, the Word], to those who believed in his name, he gave the right to become children of God—children born not of natural descent, nor of human decision or a husband's will, but born of God.'

Part of the wonder of God's grace is that the rights of Jesus—the true Son—have been extended to the adopted sons of God.[13] We are now inheritors of the family fortune. Paul tells us in Galatians 4:7 that we are sons of God and therefore heirs of God. We have received 'the full rights of sons'[14] and among other things this means that through the work of the Spirit we may now intimately address God as 'Father'.[15] I remember explaining this latter idea to my six year old daughter as we travelled somewhere in a car. I explained that because of Jesus we can now call God 'Daddy!' She was so excited by the idea that she clapped and shouted! That should be our response to this realisation too. With John we can only exclaim (1 John 3:1) 'How great is the love the Father has lavished on us, that we should be called children of God! And that is what we are!' It is not simply that we have been reconciled to our Creator, we have also been brought into God's family. Because of the work of Jesus we can address Almighty God as 'Father'. He considers us his children and loves us with an intensity and commitment that is greater than that of any earthly father.

It is time to recognise the life-changing power of the cross—

those who put their faith in the King on the cross are now the children of God.

How has the cross achieved these things for us?

How is all this possible? How can God now no longer count people's sin against them? Surely, it would not be right for him to simply close his eyes to the problem of sin; we would be extremely unhappy about a Law court judge who decided that there was no price to pay for crimes such as murder or rape. In those cases we would rightly call for justice, so how can God be righteous in not giving us our just deserts for sin? Paul in Romans 3:26 tells us that it is because God does not ignore sin—he *does* punish it—but he does so by bearing his own punishment. God is both righteous (the one who demands punishment for sin) and the one who makes people righteous (the one who provides payment for sin). In other words, it was God himself on the cross dealing with humanity's sin. The God of heaven dealt with the consequence of human sin two thousand years ago by taking the punishment *himself* on a cruel cross.

Jesus became our substitute and took our punishment

The New Testament writers repeatedly apply the words of Isaiah 53 to Jesus[16]. Words that were written hundreds of years before Jesus' birth help us to understand his death. In particular, it is clear that the one described in Isaiah 53 suffers and dies, not for his own sin, but for the sin of others. It was Jesus for us.

Look at the language of Isaiah 53:4–6:

> v.4 'Surely *he* took up *our* infirmities and carried *our* sorrows …'

v.5 '... *he* was pierced for *our* transgressions, *he* was crushed for *our* iniquities; the punishment that brought *us* peace was upon *him*, and by *his* wounds *we* are healed'

v.6 '... the LORD has laid on *him* the iniquity of *us all*.'

In other words, Jesus substituted himself for others; he took a punishment that was not his own. He experienced sorrows and suffering from God's hand, not because he was sinful, but because we are. Isaiah 53:6 continues: 'We all, like sheep, have gone astray, each of us has turned to his own way; and the LORD has laid on him the iniquity of us all.' A great exchange occurred: he received our punishment and we received peace, he received our wounds and we received God's healing.

The Apostle Peter uses the language of Isaiah 53 in 1 Peter 2:24 speaking of Jesus' sacrifice on the cross 'He himself bore our sins in his body on the tree, so that we might die to sins and live for righteousness; by his wounds you have been healed.'

The Apostle Paul speaks of Jesus 'becoming a curse for us'[17] and becoming 'sin for us'[18] even though he 'had no sin'. The innocent one 'gave himself as a ransom' on the cross.[19] The echo of the cross that resounds throughout the New Testament is that it was 'for us'. The Apostle Peter summarises what happened on the cross in 1 Peter 3:18 '... Christ died for sins once for all, the righteous for the unrighteous, to bring you to God.'

The idea of Jesus taking our place on the cross and bearing our punishment has its critics,[20] but it lies at the heart of the gospel message. Some feel embarrassed by the idea of an angry God punishing an innocent Jesus for us. Maybe you feel the same. How is it fair for God to punish an innocent Jesus for guilty people? Well, it is not ... unless the one who dies on the cross is actually God himself! If Jesus is an innocent third party who comes along, however willingly, and God punishes him for our sins, it is not fair. However, that is not what the Bible describes. It describes *God himself* taking the punishment for sin.[21] This swapping of punishment for peace, of wounds for healing is only possible if Jesus is God himself dealing with humanity's sin. Make no mistake about the fact that it was God on that cross in the darkness 2000 years ago and it was your sin and my sin that took him there.

The dangers of minimising the message of the cross

Each generation of Christians is in danger of losing sight of the priority of the cross. The way we communicate the gospel (our methods) must constantly be changing to connect effectively with our twenty-first century audience, but what we communicate (the message) must stay the same. We must never allow other messages, however worthy, to take precedence over the message of the cross, for the simple reason that *the cross is the gospel message*.

Often the danger does not come from a direct attack on the message of the cross, although there are many today who push the idea that the Gospel accounts are just a collection of helpful religious ideas without any historical roots. The greater danger, however, to the health of the contemporary church is far more subtle—the cross just gets crowded off the agenda. The preaching in the church is popular and full of engaging stories, but it is not driven by the passion of the New Testament writers to proclaim 'Jesus Christ and him crucified'.[22] Some other fad, or technique or experience has taken precedence. Sometimes the proclamation of the gospel of God's grace can even get squeezed out by an honourable desire to deal with pressing

social needs. But, whatever the reason, we must be alert to the
dangers. History is littered with the stories of churches and
Christian institutions which have come adrift from the gospel
because they minimised the message of the cross.

The material we have surveyed in this chapter should be of
fundamental importance to every true Christian. The difficulty,
however, is how to take it to heart. At times we struggle to
believe that God really means *us* when he makes these wonderful
promises of grace. We know more than any other human being
just how sinful we are; the guilt and shame of our misdeeds
seem ever before us. In the next two chapters we will explore
how God's grace addresses the ever-present problem of sin in
our daily lives and its consequences, but for now notice that
the way we are viewed in God's eyes *because of Jesus* is not
necessarily the way we feel. Our feelings rise and fall like the
waves. We have days when we see our lives with great biblical
clarity and live in humble thankfulness for all Christ has done;
on other days we are blind to the truth. As we move on we
will notice the importance of regularly speaking the truth of
the gospel into our own lives so that we can view ourselves
from God's perspective and so that we can live near the cross
of Jesus.

Endnotes

1   Matthew 27:46
2   In particular, I would highly recommend John Stott's classic *The Cross of Christ*.
3   Hebrews 2:14–15
4   Colossians 2:13
5   2 Corinthians 5:19
6   English Standard Version
7   Notice that the cross has not only achieved *personal reconciliation* but also what we
    might call *cosmic reconciliation*. Christ has reconciled 'all things' (Colossians 1:20).
    Ephesians 2 also describes the 'horizontal' dimension of reconciliation between
    Jews and Gentiles. Those who were once divided and at enmity are now reconciled
    through the cross (vv.14–18)

8   1 Corinthians 15
9   See for example Philippians 1:21–24; 3:20
10 1 Corinthians 15:50–57
11 John 17:3
12 John 8:35
13 This is not intended to exclude women. In the New Testament, believers, both male and female, are given the status of 'sons of God' due to the fact that it was the sons who received the family inheritance, not the daughters. Although this idea goes against the grain in our gender-inclusive society, if we understand why the New Testament uses this language we can rejoice in the fact that we are sons of God (whether we are male or female).
14 Galatians 4:5
15 Obviously, our understanding of the word 'father' is informed by our own experience of our earthly, sinful fathers. Some of us have a positive view of this relationship if our father was a loving one, whereas others have a negative view because of abusive fathers. We must understand that in God we have the Perfect Father (Matthew 7:9–11).
16 John Stott estimates, for example, that eight of the twelve verses of Isaiah 53 are quoted in connection with Jesus' ministry. J. Stott, *The Cross of Christ* (Leicester: IVP, 1986), p.145.
17 Galatians 3:13
18 2 Corinthians 5:21
19 1 Timothy 2:6
20 Even within the evangelical world there has been a relatively recent controversy over the caricaturing of Jesus' death on the cross as 'Cosmic child abuse', Steve Chalke and Alan Mann, *The Lost Message of Jesus* (Grand Rapids: Zondervan, 2003)
21 See, for example, 2 Corinthians 5:19 and Galatians 1:3–5
22 1 Corinthians 2:2

4
Our daily struggle

The problem of sin

This story would not look out of place on the front pages of the tabloids. It would feature with attached photographs of the beautiful wife and the shamefaced celebrity. The journalists would take great pleasure in sensationalising the lurid details: a passionate sexual encounter that destroyed a marriage, a powerful man, lustful looks, sexual intrigue, deceit and lies, adultery, drunken parties, the misuse of government resources, murder on the battlefield, and a national cover-up that is finally exposed. It is not the sort of story you expect to find *in the Bible*, but there it is.

It was spring time. This was the time, according to 2 Samuel 11:1, when 'kings go off to war', but King David was not fulfilling his royal duties by leading the Israelite armies this year. He had sent Joab, his army chief, in his place to fight against the Ammonites. David had decided to stay at home. Maybe he felt his kingdom was secure and that it was his prerogative not to go; maybe he felt he had done his fair share of fighting, but whatever the reason this spring the king was taking it easy in Jerusalem whilst his troops defended the realm. That was when he saw her. David apparently could not sleep one night and was walking up on the palace roof. As he stood in the dark he saw a beautiful woman bathing, and he wanted her. The problem was that she was another man's wife. Bathsheba was the wife of Uriah the Hittite, who ironically was away fighting in David's army. David made discreet enquiries about who she was but on finding out the truth he did not seem deterred by the fact that she was already married. The king was probably quite used to getting his own way. He called for Bathsheba to come to his bedroom and he slept with her.

Maybe David had intended this to be a one night stand. The problem was, however, that Bathsheba became pregnant. This meant that David needed to cover his tracks. He recalled Uriah from the battle-front under the guise of getting up-to-date information about the war. In doing so, he hoped that Uriah would go home, sleep with his wife, and after fudging the dates a little, Uriah would think himself a proud father. But Uriah would not go home. He was on active duty. Apparently he was an honourable man who cared deeply about his army colleagues stuck out on the front line and so he determined that he would not enjoy his home comforts whilst his friends were in danger of their lives. Despite David's repeated attempts to get him to go home, Uriah decided to remain at the palace until he was redeployed. The king even attempted to get him drunk in the hope he might stumble home to sleep with his wife in a drunken stupor.

Finally, David resorted to 'plan b' in an attempt to hide his own shortcomings. He arranged with Joab for Uriah to be sent to the frontline and placed where the battle raged most fiercely. Then David instructed the Israelite army to withdraw, leaving him undefended, so that he might be killed. Well, David's self-serving plan worked. He successfully managed to deal with his embarrassing problem. Everything had been discretely dealt with, and after an appropriate period of mourning David took Bathsheba home to be his wife. 2 Samuel 11 ends however with ominous words: '... the thing David had done displeased the LORD.' The Living God had been watching. David, the king who had once been described as 'a man after God's own heart'[1] had disobeyed God and God was not pleased. He had broken at least five of the 'ten commandments': he had murdered, he had committed adultery, he had stolen, he had lied and he had coveted his neighbour's wife. Maybe David thought he had got away with it, but the story was far from over. This sin was to have far-reaching consequences in his life.[2] God sent the prophet Nathan to David to confront him over his sin and David was brought to realise that nothing is hidden from God.

It would be so easy for us to stand in judgement upon David, just as the tabloids take great pleasure in exposing the shame of others. We may well consider ourselves more righteous than him because we have not sinned *so badly*, but is that actually true? Can we really claim to be any better than David? Can we point a finger at him without one pointing back at us? Our sin, although probably not as public as David's, is just as dirty and outrageous in God's eyes. Despite the wonderful achievements of the cross that we looked at in the last chapter, the truth is that *even Christians*—those who have been declared righteous in God's eyes—still have daily struggles with sin. The war against sin has been decisively won at the cross but there are still many battles to fight before the victory is complete. Sin no longer enslaves us as it once did before the cross, but we still live in a sin-damaged world and sin continually draws us away from God. We've got a fight on our hands if we want to live for Jesus.

God's verdict about our lives

Fundamental to a true understanding of who we are as human beings is an acceptance of the Bible's verdict that we are all sinners. The Apostle Paul, for example, writes in Romans 3:10–12, 23:

> 'There is no one righteous, not even one; there is no one who understands, no one who seeks God. All have turned away, they have together become worthless; there is no one who does good, not even one … for all have sinned and fall short of the glory of God …'

Jesus tells us that the source of sin in our lives is our hearts (Mark 7:21–22): '… from within, out of men's hearts, come evil thoughts, sexual immorality, theft, murder, adultery, greed, malice, deceit, lewdness, envy, slander, arrogance and folly.' This means that even if we were somehow able to tidy up our lives on the outside, without God's help, we would never be able to deal with the internal problem of our sin-sick hearts.[3] The problem is not just that we commit acts that displease God; it is also that we fail to love God and love others in the way we should.[4] We not only sin by doing wrong, we sin by failing to do what is right. The Apostle Paul is writing as a Christian when he acknowledges that 'nothing good dwells' in him. He has 'the desire to do what is right, but not the ability to carry it out' (Romans 7:18).[5] In the end Paul recognises that only Jesus can save him from this deadly problem.[6] The same is true for us—we are sinners in need of a Saviour. We need the cross of Jesus, not just for sins committed before we became Christians, but also for those we commit as believers. We'll see in the next chapter that God's Spirit is at work in our lives making us more like Jesus day by day, but perfection is not something we will experience in this life. The day when sin is eradicated from our lives forever is still in the future. We must face up to the facts. Christians are *forgiven* sinners who love God and who desire to turn away from sin, but we are sinners nevertheless and we daily struggle with sin. It is because this is true that the words of Psalm 51 are so helpful for us. This psalm is David's response to God after 'the Bathsheba incident', where he confesses his sin and pleads for forgiveness. In Psalm 51 David stands where we need to stand on a regular basis—confessing our sin to the Living God and admitting that we have nowhere else to go for forgiveness.

Forgive me

'Have mercy on me, O God, according to your unfailing love; according to your great compassion blot out my transgressions. Wash away all my iniquity and cleanse me from my sin.' (Psalm 51:1–2)

David's is a passionate prayer for forgiveness. He pleads with God to hit the delete button and take his sin away. His starting point is the mercy, compassion and unfailing love of God[7] and he calls on God to act according to these aspects of his character. He knows that he doesn't deserve forgiveness and that God has every right to be angry with him, but he cries to him for mercy. He asks God to wash away his sin so that he might be 'whiter than snow' (v.7). It is those same characteristics of God that we depend upon for forgiveness. We can only plead with God for forgiveness on the basis of his gracious character because our sins against him are indefensible. There is nowhere else to go with our sin except the cross of Jesus where God's grace and mercy are supremely displayed to an unworthy world. It is because of Jesus' blood spilt there that we can be washed from sin and can be 'whiter than snow'.

In this psalm David realises the extent to which his sin has messed everything up. He talks about feeling 'crushed' by God (v.8) and speaks of his longing to experience 'joy and gladness' once more. He calls on God to hide his face from his sins (v.9). Clearly, David understands something of the true horror of his sin. Unfortunately, it is rare for us as Christians to recognise the same in our own lives. We fail to grasp how much our sin offends a holy God. We dismiss it as unimportant. We are quick with the excuses and slow to contemplate the ugliness of our fallen nature. However, there is an urgent need for us to recognise 'the sinfulness of sin'.

As a Christian from a middle class family it would not cross my mind to steal from someone, or to use God's name as a swear word, or to knowingly lie. On the outside I look fairly respectable, but I have many hidden struggles with sin. I struggle to love God above all things so that I find my comfort and security in him alone. I struggle to be what I am not naturally— a loving husband and father. I struggle to feel a genuine love for others who are not part of my immediate circle. I struggle with critical attitudes that lead me to gossip about people behind their backs. I struggle with my own selfishness that causes me to manipulate situations for my own ends. I struggle to keep my mind pure. And the list goes on. These are not 'high profile' sins; they go largely unnoticed by others, but when I sin in these more subtle ways they are no less sinful than more obvious sinful acts like murder or committing adultery. I am so familiar with these sins that I often think of them as somehow acceptable and fail to see their ugliness. But when I commit sins such as these I choose to forget that these were exactly the sins that caused Jesus to be nailed to a cross for me.

We must acknowledge the truth as Christians that even our best thoughts and actions are shot through with all sorts of sinful desires and motivations. Like David, we must recognize the true horror our sin. That is the first step to forgiveness.

Against you, you only, have I sinned

'For I know my transgressions, and my sin is always before me. Against you, you only, have I sinned and done what is evil in your sight, so that you are proved right when you speak and justified when you judge.' (Psalm 51:3–4)

These words are surprising. We could write a list of people David had sinned against, but as he acknowledges his sin he says to God 'Against you, you only have I sinned and done what is evil in your sight ...' David recognizes that ultimately sin is an offence to a holy God. It is true that our sin hurts us, and it hurts others, but ultimately it hurts God. Sin is breaking *his* righteous laws.[8]

There is a popular myth going around that suggests that the worst 'sin' you can commit is being found out. It is suggested that what people do in their private lives is their own business; it is only when it becomes public knowledge that it becomes a problem. However, that idea is inconsistent with the teaching of the Bible because it assumes that sin is primarily 'horizontal'. In other words, that it only becomes a problem when it becomes an offence to others, but David acknowledges here in Psalm 51 that sin is primarily 'vertical'—it is an offence to God. David did the best he could to cover up his sin but there were still many human spectators, and ultimately he was brought to realize that God had been watching his life. God is always watching. Whether others discover our sin is not the point. He sees to the heart. We may successfully hide our sin from others, but our evil is always done in *his* sight.

David knew that there were no excuses for what he had done (v.4). Nowadays we are quick to play the role of victim, blaming our upbringing or the government or the school system, but David freely acknowledges his guilt. When the Righteous Judge of the world passed judgement, David knew that his judgement was right. There were no excuses. In fact, David acknowledges that his sinful nature was part of his makeup from birth, even from the time he was conceived: 'Surely I was sinful at birth, sinful from the time my mother conceived me.' (v.5) David shared the curse of humanity that stretches all the way back to Adam and Eve (just as we do today) but that in itself was no excuse for his rebellion: 'Surely you desire truth in the inner parts; you teach me wisdom in the inmost place.' (v.6) He knew how he should be living his life. He knew what was right, but he had broken God's laws. God desired truth and wisdom, but David had chosen lies and foolishness.

We need to realise the same. There are no excuses we can give and nothing we can do to make up for our rebellion against God. As we have already seen our only hope is to throw ourselves on the mercy and unfailing love and compassion of our God revealed in the cross of Jesus. There is nowhere else to go with our sin problem.

Create in me a pure heart

'Create in me a pure heart, O God, and renew a steadfast spirit within me. Do not cast me from your presence or take your Holy Spirit from me. Restore to me the joy of your salvation and grant me a willing spirit, to sustain me.' (Psalm 51:10–12)

David asked God to create a pure heart within him because he realised that his sin was a problem of the heart. It was internal, not external. It was not just a problem of what he had done, but rather of who he was. He needed God to change him on the inside; to purify his heart and renew his spirit so that he would have the inner strength to do what was right. He longed for his joy to be restored in God and in his saving acts. It was true that David had sinned, but it was also true that he loved God and he enjoyed a friendship with him. He loved the presence of God's Spirit in his life. David was afraid that his sin had spoilt this relationship and so he asks God not to cast him from his presence and not to take his Holy Spirit away from him. That fear was probably based on what he had seen in the life of Saul, the previous king of Israel. Saul had been rejected by God as king and 1 Samuel 16:14 tells us that: '... the Spirit of the Lord had departed from Saul, and an evil spirit from the Lord tormented him.' David had seen this first hand. He had been called in to bring Saul some relief by playing the harp when he was tortured and in despair. Clearly David did not want that to happen to him. He knew he had sinned, but he loved God and he knew that life was empty without him, and so he pleaded with God for their relationship to be restored.

As Christians we can all relate to David's words here—we easily wander away from God into sin and that sin spoils our relationship with God. Sin takes away our joy in Christ. It causes distance between us and our God. Of course, what happened to King Saul cannot happen to us. God will never remove his Spirit from us. That is one of the privileges of being a 'new covenant' believer—a Christian. The Holy Spirit has taken up residence in our lives and God will not withdraw that wonderful privilege. However, Ephesians 4:30 informs us that we can 'grieve the Holy Spirit of God' by our sin. This implies that we can damage our relationship with God as Christians when we continue in sin. So, we need to follow David's lead in Psalm 51. We must confess our sins before God and in addition claim the victory of the cross in our lives.

I have found the following prayer helpful in asking God to clean up my life:

Almighty God,
to whom all hearts are open,
all desires known,
and from whom no secrets are hidden:
cleanse the thoughts of our hearts
by the inspiration of Your Holy Spirit,
that we may perfectly love you,
and worthily magnify your holy name,
through Christ our Lord. Amen.[9]

One of the exercises I've carried out with my students at Namibia Evangelical Theological Seminary is to get them to write down what they consider to be their worst sin on a piece of paper. I've noticed that the students look nervous as they do this and carefully fold their paper so that others can't see it. We do this exercise, however, as an act of confession before God. Finally, each of us (lecturer included) brings our paper forward and we put it through a paper shredder so that it is destroyed and never identified with us again. This symbolizes what Christ has done with our sin on the cross—it is gone forever through his one mighty act of sacrifice! However, that objective reality needs to be appropriated in our Christian lives day by day. I frequently claim the promise of 1 John 1:8–9 for my own life:

> 'If we claim to be without sin, we deceive ourselves and the truth is not in us. If we confess our sins, he is faithful and just and will forgive us our sins and purify us from all unrighteousness.'

I am so thankful those words are in the Bible! They show me how I can experience God's cleansing in my life and they allow me to forgive myself because I have been forgiven by God. The words of the hymn[10] below capture that truth well:

When Satan tempts me to despair,
And shows me of the guilt within,
Upward I look and see Him there
Who made an end to all my sin.
Because the sinless Saviour died,
My guilty soul is counted free
For God the Just was satisfied
To look on Him and pardon me

Two unhelpful responses
We have been honest in this chapter about the fact that Christians

are sinners. This is an unpleasant truth and one that we don't readily like to own up to. Sometimes when confronted with this truth Christians go to extremes, rather than embracing God's grace on offer at the cross.

Living with condemnation

The first unhelpful response we can make to the realisation that we are sinners is to live with condemnation because of our sin. We have all done things we are deeply ashamed of, and sometimes we think that God could never forgive us for those things. As we think about our sin we realise that it is inexcusable and we feel condemned. But we must remember that all sin is inexcusable! If it were something that could easily be brushed aside then the cross of Jesus would not have been necessary. Often the problem is that we can't forgive ourselves and therefore we find it hard to believe that Jesus has really forgiven that sin that still stings. But here we must face up to the objective reality of the cross—Jesus *has* taken our sin away and Christians must not live as if he has not! Of course, sin has consequences (as it did for David) but we must hold on to the truth we've already examined that there is now 'no condemnation for those who are in Christ Jesus'.[11] This is not a misprint in your Bible—it says *no* condemnation. Not even a little bit. None. Because of the cross of Jesus our sin is not held against us. We have no need to live anymore with feelings of condemnation because of our sin.

Living with pretence

The second unhelpful response we can make to the realisation that we are sinners is to live pretending that sin is no longer a problem for us and that we are not struggling with sin.

Some Bible teachers suggest that it is possible for Christians to be perfect in this life. They reject the idea that Christians are sinners. They suggest that Christians live 'in victory' over sin because of the cross, and therefore can live sinless lives. However, perfection is not something that the Bible promises to Christians in the 'here and now'. Although the Bible does teach that Christ has won a full victory over sin at the cross, and that Christians can make great progress in holiness, this view confuses the promises of God for heaven with this life. It also does not square with reality. A little time spent with the wife and children of someone who claimed perfection would probably be enough to discredit their claims!

Sometimes we live with pretence over sin because we have become a little self-righteous as Christians. We start to fool ourselves that actually we are better than we really are. We start to believe that God has accepted us into his family because we were worthy in some way of such an honour! However, that is not what the Bible teaches. It tells us that God did not choose us for salvation because we were good. Jesus died for sinners.[12] No-one is good enough to earn God's favour.[13] That is why we need to give up our pretence and acknowledge the truth that we are sinners in need of God's grace.

In this chapter we have faced up to the reality of our daily struggle with sin, but in the next one we will see that Christians are given daily grace through the gospel to deal with such sin. God has not left us alone in our struggle. He is at work in our lives by his Spirit and his grace makes all the difference.

Endnotes

1   1 Samuel 13:14
2   See 2 Samuel 12
3   Jeremiah 17:9

4 Matthew 22:37–40

5 English Standard Version

6 Romans 7:24–25

7 Exodus 34:6–7

8 That was why the religious leaders of Jesus' day were outraged at his suggestion that he had authority to forgive sins (Mark 2:5, 10). To their ears it was blasphemous because 'Who can forgives sins but God alone?' (Mark 2:7) and, of course, their reasoning was correct—forgiving sins *is* God's prerogative. What they failed to see was that Jesus had God's authority to forgive sins because he was God become flesh.

9 The Alternative Prayer Book of the Church of England (1980)

10. Verse 2 of the hymn 'Before the throne of God above'. Lyrics by Charitie Lees Bancroft (1841–1923)

11. Romans 8:1

12. Romans 5:8

13. Mark 10:18. The only exception is Jesus—the one who was without sin (Hebrews 4:15)

5

The difference grace makes

Living in the light of the gospel

My sister once noticed the following words pinned to the noticeboard of the hospital where she worked: 'Due to government cutbacks the light at the end of the tunnel has been extinguished until further notice!'

We may well feel the same way about our lives. The problem is not government cutbacks; the problem is sin. We despair about the hold it seems to have on our lives and we wonder where the light is at the end of the tunnel. There is hope however. Although the Bible leaves us in no doubt about the evil of our own hearts, it also leaves us in no doubt about where we find hope. It is true that we have a daily struggle with sin, but God's grace is greater than our worst sin! This is how the Apostle Paul continues in Romans 3:23–25a, having acknowledged the devastating problem of sin:

'… all have sinned and fall short of the glory of God, and are justified by his grace as a gift, through the redemption that is in Christ Jesus, whom God put forward as a propitiation by his blood, to be received by faith.'[1]

That is the full story. Our lives don't measure up to God's perfect standards, but through faith in Jesus we can be justified (declared 'not guilty' before God) and redeemed (rescued from sin and for God). Notice that Paul says that this has all been given as a gracious gift of God and is only possible because of Christ's blood spilt on the cross for us. The cross is the very definition of love; it is the place where God's grace overwhelms the darkness of our hearts forever. 'In this is love, not that we have loved God, but that he loved us and sent his Son to be the propitiation for our sins.' (1 John 4:10)[2]

God is at work

Although we must recognise the presence of sin in our lives as Christians we must also recognise a greater presence: God is ever at work in our lives by his Spirit and day by day he is making us more like Jesus. This process of being made holy (or sanctified) covers the past, the present and the future according to the New Testament.

It is biblically true to say that the Christian *has already* been made holy. Paul reminds the Corinthian Christians about the evil lives they used to lead before becoming Christians and then describes in 1 Corinthians 6:11 the difference God's grace makes: 'But you were washed, you were sanctified, you were justified in the name of the Lord Jesus Christ and by the Spirit of our God.'

It is also biblically true to say the Christian *is being* made holy. The writer of Hebrews states that 'by one sacrifice [Jesus] has made perfect forever those who are being made holy' (Hebrews 10:14). Paul writes on the same theme in 2 Corinthians 3:18, and there describes the Spirit's work in our lives as that of making us more like Jesus: 'And we ... are being transformed into his likeness with ever-increasing glory, which comes from the Lord, who is the Spirit.' In Galatians 5:22–23 Paul describes the characteristics of God ('the fruit of the Spirit') that are being reproduced in our lives by the work of the Spirit: '... the fruit of the Spirit is love, joy, peace, patience, kindness, goodness, faithfulness, gentleness and self-control.'

Holiness is also part of our future as Christians. The Bible tells us that the Christian *will be* made holy. Paul prays these words for the Thessalonian Christians (1 Thessalonians 3:13): 'May he strengthen your hearts so that you will be blameless and holy in the presence of our God and Father when our Lord Jesus comes with all his holy ones.'

Elsewhere, Paul describes the church as the 'bride of Christ' (Ephesians 5:27) which Christ, the bridegroom, will one day 'present ... to himself as a radiant church, without stain or wrinkle or any other blemish, but holy and blameless.' Jude (v.24) says something similar when he speaks of Christians being presented 'before his glorious presence without fault and with great joy'.

It is a bit like going out on a date with a new boyfriend or girlfriend. When you fall in love with someone you take your meetings extremely seriously. You anticipate them with great excitement. You prepare yourself for the day when you will be together. If you are a woman you choose the right perfume, put on your make-up, style your hair, and then change your clothes three times before you are happy that you look alright!

If you are a man you do something outrageous like have a shower, or put on after-shave, or even iron your shirt! When you meet the one you love you want to look as 'faultless' as possible, and you revel in the tremendous joy of just being together. That maybe gives us a small insight into another meeting that we should anticipate with great excitement—the day when we are brought into the presence of the Living God! The wonderful truth about that day, however, is that God himself will have prepared us for it through the work of his Son on the cross. We will be faultless. We will be totally clean and ready to meet God. The Bible promises that this will be a day of tremendous joy. That is our future as Christians. We will be unstained, unwrinkled and unblemished in God's glorious presence.

That day of perfection, however, is still a future one, so how then are we to live in the meantime? Well, we are called by God to pursue holiness. It strikes me that there are two ways that we can wait as Christians for that future to be revealed. The first way is what we might call 'passive waiting'. That's the sort of waiting that you do as you await the arrival of a bus. You stand at the bus stop; you read the newspaper; you day-dream. In other words, you do nothing of any significance. But the Bible does not call us to be passively waiting for eternity; rather it calls us to 'active waiting'. That is the sort of waiting that you do as you await the arrival of a new baby. There are all sorts of things which need to be done to get ready for that great day. You paint the small room. You borrow every piece of baby equipment you can lay your hands on from your friends and family, and you buy a shelf full of nappies and baby wipes. There are important preparations to make. The same is true as we wait for eternity. We must pursue with every fibre of our being in this life what we will become in the next—to become more like Jesus.

The final activity of God's Spirit I want to note here is that he empowers us to live as Christians and he enlightens us so that we can understand how much we are loved by Christ. Paul prays for the Ephesian Christians with these words (Ephesians 3:16–19):

> 'I pray that out of his glorious riches he may strengthen you with power through his Spirit in your inner being, so that Christ may dwell in your hearts through faith. And I pray that you, being rooted and established in love, may have power, together with all the saints, to grasp how wide and long and high and deep is the love of Christ, and to know this love that surpasses knowledge ...'

We may well feel weak and sinful, but God is powerful and he is at work within us by his Spirit combating sin and its destructive effects. He will help us to turn from sin. He will help us to be more like Jesus each day, and he will help us to understand how much we are loved by Jesus. The Spirit reveals to us the wonder of God's grace in the gospel. He shows us day by day that Christ's love for us is wider and longer and higher and deeper than we could ever have imagined. He helps us to see that we are loved by Christ with an intensity and a magnitude that is beyond our wildest dreams. It is this understanding that gives us the motivation to keep struggling with our sin.

Welcome to the partnership!

We have already seen that God's work in our lives does not

mean that we are without responsibility as Christians. The Bible shows us that we have a responsibility to pursue holiness. God tells his people to 'Be holy, because I am holy' (1 Peter 1:16). God's sovereign work in our lives does not preclude our personal responsibility. The Christian life is a partnership[3] between the Living God and us. It is an unequal one admittedly,[4] but it is a partnership nevertheless. Look for example at Philippians 2:12b–13 where Paul tells the Christians in Philippi to: '… continue to work out your salvation with fear and trembling, for it is God who works in you to will and to act according to his good purpose.'

Paul makes it plain that Christians must work out their salvation *and* at the same time that it is God who is at work in them fulfilling his good purpose. Human responsibility and Divine sovereignty are taught side by side in the Bible. *God* is at work within you making you holy but *you* need to seek holiness. Notice Paul's teaching, for example, in Colossians 3:5–8 and the commands there that imply personal responsibility in our Christian lives:

'*Put to death*, therefore, whatever belongs to your earthly nature: sexual immorality, impurity, lust, evil desires and greed, which is idolatry. Because of these, the wrath of God is coming. You used to walk in these ways, in the life you once lived. But now you must *rid yourselves* of all such things as these: anger, rage, malice, slander, and filthy language from your lips.'

Likewise, Peter calls Christians in 2 Peter 3:14 in the light of Christ's return to: '… *make every effort* to be found spotless, blameless and at peace with [God].' Paul writes in 2 Corinthians 7:1 '… dear friends, *let us purify ourselves* from everything that contaminates body and spirit, perfecting holiness out of reverence for God.'

God is making us holy, but we are in partnership with him now and we have a responsibility to pursue holiness.

There is no other price to pay for sin

I was at a restaurant recently with friends who secretly paid the bill for the meal. My wife and I were expecting to pay for our share, but when we had finished eating we discovered that the bill had already been covered. As we gathered our things together it took me a few moments to realise that I was free to go from the restaurant because the price had been paid. It would have been ridiculous for me to go to the waiter and demand to pay for a meal that has already been paid for. I could do nothing but accept the generous gift of my friends. It is the same with Jesus' work on the cross. The Bible makes it clear that there is nothing to add to what Jesus has already done.

The book of Hebrews shows us that Jesus' sacrifice on the cross does what the Old Testament sacrifices could never do— it deals with our sin once and for all time. The writer of Hebrews tells us that the sacrifices of the Old Testament were not able to 'clear the conscience of the worshipper' (Hebrews 9:9). They were temporary, they needed to be repeated time and time again, and they didn't finally deal with the problem of sin. They were simply shadows of the real thing.

Christ's sacrifice, however, is the real thing. It has eternal consequences and it is complete.[5] The writer of Hebrews pictures Christ as the priest who makes the perfect sacrifice and then sits at the right hand of God to await the completion of God's plans through that one act of sacrifice (Hebrews 10:12) '...

when this priest had offered for all time one sacrifice for sins, he sat down at the right hand of God.'

In summary we see that: '... [Christ] has appeared once for all at the end of the ages to do away with sin by the sacrifice of himself.' (Hebrews 9:26). Through one mighty act of sacrifice our sin has been dealt with fully and finally. If we are Christians there is no other price to pay for our sin—Christ has done it all. We can do nothing except gratefully receive his grace. This full and free forgiveness has everything to do with him and nothing to do with us. So when we are tempted to despair about our sin, let's remember what Christ has done for us—our sin past, present, and future has been dealt with at the cross.

Jesus has taken away our shame

Hebrews 12:2 tells us that '... for the joy that was set before him [Jesus] endured the cross, despising the shame, and is seated at the right hand of the throne of God.'[6]

In other words Jesus willingly endured the shame, the humiliation, of the cross for us. The cross itself is a graphic picture of what it means to be humiliated. Public execution like crucifixion was calculated to be dehumanising and bring shame to those who were executed and their families. However, the humiliation of the cross did not come simply from the fact that Jesus died an undignified death as if he were a common criminal—what we might call *social humiliation*.[7] This is often what we think of when we think of shame—we do not want to be shown up and ashamed *before others* for our wrongdoing. Rather in the New Testament shame is often humiliation associated with sin and judgement. It is being shown up and ashamed *before God* for our wrongdoing—what we might call *sinful humiliation*.[8] Well, it is this sinful humiliation that Jesus willingly endured on the cross—even though he was sinless. He bore the shame associated with our sin and he removed it from us forever, so that by trusting in him we will never be put to shame (Romans 10:11). We will no longer experience God's punishment. We will not be like Adam and Eve pathetically trying to cover our shame on that final day (Genesis 3:7) because Jesus has taken our shame away.

Jesus has taken away our fear

We who once aroused God's anger because of our sin had good reason to fear the Living God and his punishment, but now because of the cross that fear has been taken away. Because Jesus has opened up a way for us back into God's holy presence through the sacrifice of his life, the writer to the Hebrews calls Christians to 'draw near to God with a sincere heart in full assurance of faith, having our hearts sprinkled to cleanse us from a guilty conscience and having our bodies washed with pure water.' (Hebrews 10:22)

The picture is one of being cleaned up on the inside and the outside through the work of the cross so that we might come into God's presence with confidence and without fear. Earlier in Hebrews Christians are encouraged that Jesus, our sinless High Priest in heaven, is able to understand us in the frailty of our humanity and therefore we are able to 'approach the throne of grace with confidence, so that we may receive mercy and find grace to help us in our time of need.' (Hebrews 4:16) We can now approach the Living God with boldness because of Jesus, and it is there at the throne of grace that we can experience his mercy and grace for our lives. We are not called to come into God's presence with fear and trembling anymore, God's forgiven people are called to come into his presence with confidence because of Jesus.

Repent and believe again … and again … and again

In chapter 1 we noted Jesus' twin commands of Mark 1:15 to 'Repent and believe the good news!' This is the response we first make to the gospel. It is through repenting and believing (by the grace and power of God) that we become Christians. However, we need to be aware that these are not just one-off responses that we make to Christ so that we are brought into God's family; they are actually the responses Christians need to make daily to the gospel. We might think that repenting and believing are for non-Christians. Once we have become Christians we can move on from this basic teaching to something else, but that is not what the Bible teaches. The commands of Jesus from Mark 1:15 in the original Greek are in a tense that shows that they are to be continuous responses, rather than a one-off response.[9] The repentance and faith when we first turn to Christ are to be the first of a lifetime of similar responses. They are not just the responses we make to God to *begin* the Christian life, but they are the regular responses that are commanded of us as we *continue* in the Christian life. In fact, Jesus calls us to radical repentance. In Matthew 5:29–30 Jesus tells his disciples in the context of teaching about lustful looks: 'If your right eye causes you to sin, gouge it out and throw it away. It is better for you to lose one part of your body than for your whole body to be thrown into hell. And if your right hand causes you to sin, cut it off and throw it away. It is better for you to lose one part of your body than for your whole body to go into hell.'

Although there have been Christians in church history who

have taken Jesus' words literally here by removing body parts[10] to demonstrate their repentance, most have understood Jesus to be referring to the extreme importance of 'cutting out' sin and its causes in our lives.

Nowadays that sort of radical repentance seems alien to us because we quickly overlook sin in our lives, but Jesus calls us to root out sin from our lives and 'cut it out'. Following Jesus should mean that, on occasion, we walk out of the cinema before the end of the movie because we realise that it is leading us into sin. Following Jesus should mean that we make three of the most difficult steps of our lives to walk over to the TV and turn it off, or raise a heavy finger to hit the off button on the remote control. Following Jesus should mean throwing novels in the bin half-read, cancelling our subscription for that magazine or putting controls on our computer so that we cannot access those websites anymore. Sin is not something to be played with. It leads us by the nose to hell. Every day we must turn to God from sin—even at great personal cost. Every day we must put our faith in the Jesus of the cross. The Bible tells us to make an active daily response to the gospel.

Keep your eyes on Jesus

Jesus instituted a meal (what we call 'Communion' or the 'Lord's supper') for his disciples just before his death, where they were to break bread and drink wine 'in remembrance' of him.[11] This fact shows us the necessity of keeping the cross central to our thinking as Christians. Clearly Jesus knows us better than we know ourselves; sinful human beings quickly forget the wonder of the gospel, and through the Communion meal we are brought to remember his great sacrifice on our behalf 'until he comes'.[12] However, it is not only during this meal that we must reflect on the cross. It must become the focus of our daily lives. It is only as the gospel message is understood and applied on a regular basis to our lives that we will see the need to repent and believe. The writer to the Hebrews calls Christians who are in danger of '*drifting away*' from the gospel[13] to live with their thoughts[14] and their eyes fixed on Jesus (Hebrews 12:1b–2a): 'let us run with endurance the race that is set before us, looking to Jesus, the founder and perfecter of our faith …'[15]

Earlier in Hebrews the Christians are instructed to 'encourage one another daily [with the message of Christ[16]], as long as it is still called Today, so that none of you may be hardened by sin's deceitfulness.' (Hebrews 3:13)

It is by looking at Jesus and reminding ourselves (and each other) of the gospel that we are able to live from God's grace, and it is living from God's grace which protects us from sin (as we will see in the next chapter). Every day of our lives we need to remind ourselves of what Jesus has done for us on the cross, because it is only as we do that we will get our lives in perspective. In reminding ourselves of the gospel in this way we recognise again that we don't need to live with condemnation. We don't need to live as if the cross of Jesus never happened. We also see the hollowness of pretence. We know we are sinners. We don't need to pretend otherwise, but by keeping our eyes on Jesus we find help to resist sin.

The wonder of God's grace is that I am a *forgiven* sinner and God is at work in me by his Spirit, and one day the sin I struggle with constantly will be a thing of the past as I meet Jesus face to face. The cross is not just the starting point of my Christian life but it is the heartbeat of my Christian life. My sin was nailed to that cross with Jesus and now my life will never be the same again. I live for him now. The Apostle Paul writes (Galatians 2:20): 'I have been crucified with Christ and I no longer live, but Christ lives in me. The life I live in the body, I live by faith in the Son of God, who loved me and gave himself for me.'

Endnotes

1   English Standard Version
2   English Standard Version
3   In particular, the Bible speaks about 'partnership' or 'fellowship' with the Holy Spirit (2 Corinthians 13:14; Philippians 2:1)
4   God's love and power in our lives are of a different order to our own. See for example Romans 8:35–39; Ephesians 3:20–21 and Jude 24–25
5   Hebrews 9:26
6   English Standard Version
7   See Luke 14:9 for an example of this
8   See 2 Corinthians 4:2; Philippians 3:19; Jude 1:13; Revelation 3:18
9   'Both verbs [i.e. repent and believe] in Greek are present imperatives, that is, they enjoin living in a condition of repentance and belief as opposed to momentary acts. Repentance and belief cannot be applied to certain areas of life but not to others; rather, they lay claim to the total allegiance of believers.' James R. Edwards, *The Gospel according to Mark* (*Pillar New Testament Commentary*) (Leicester: Apollos, 2002)
10 Origen, for example, castrated himself
11 Luke 22:19; 1 Corinthians 11:24
12 1 Corinthians 11:26
13 Hebrews 2:1
14 Hebrews 3:1. See also Hebrews 12:3
15 English Standard Version
16 See Hebrews 3:14

Section 3: Grace Reapplied

6
Deadly desires

The dangers of legalism and lawlessness

When my eldest son Benjamin was four years old a small crisis rocked our household. We had spent part of the day shopping and had returned home to find that 'Puppy' was missing! Puppy, you need to realise, was not a real dog, but a faded blue cuddly toy, which had lost almost all its stuffing and had been mended and washed more times than we cared to remember. It had been Benjamin's companion since he was a baby. He would not go anywhere without Puppy and in particular he would not go to sleep without his Puppy. For Benjamin losing his stuffed toy was like losing a family member. For his mum and dad losing his stuffed toy meant losing sleep for many nights whilst trying to comfort a distraught child.

We turned the house up-side down. Friends came to help. I considered going back to the shopping mall to question shop assistants and search bins. The house was turned the right way up again and finally, much to everyone's relief, Puppy was located in a suitcase. Benjamin had packed it away for a trip we were going on and had forgotten what he had done. That was the day when we realised just how important Puppy was to our son!

It is quite unlikely that many of us have an on-going 'love affair' with a stuffed toy. Hopefully that is a childhood obsession, but what are the things that we obsess about as adults? Think for a moment about the following personal questions: *What do you value most? What is your greatest love? What is at the centre of your life?*

Here are some of the answers you might give. Many people would place family at the top of the list; others would mention their education, or their years of expertise in a particular field or even their status in society. We can become easily impressed by titles such as Doctor or Professor or Reverend, and even more so when *we* own them! Some of us speak with passion about our jobs, or our holidays or our friends. Some might even tell us honestly of the importance of their house or their car. And yet we know as Christians that our answer is meant to be different. We know that we should reply that our greatest love is our relationship with God through Jesus Christ. But what is the *honest* answer? What do you value most? What is your greatest love? What is at the centre of your life?

It is good for us to review these questions from time to time as Christians so that we can re-evaluate our Christian lives. What really lies at the centre? It is on this very issue that the Apostle Paul challenges us to rethink our priorities in Philippians 3. In this chapter he warns of two deadly desires—two sinful patterns of living—that can damage our Christian lives. The first is that of legalism (3:1–11) and the second is the opposing danger of lawlessness (3:18–19). He tells the Philippians that the Christian life is one that must be centred on Christ and his grace. He warns that their Christianity must not become a religion of rules at one extreme or a selfish pursuit of pleasure at the other. In the final two chapters of this book we will see that these dangers are not simply first century problems, but actually ones that can derail our Christian faith in the twenty-first century. We must look for the danger signs in our own lives. Paul's teaching in Philippians 3 describes three ways of living, two of which are bogus. He talks about the Lord-centred life, the Law-centred life and the Lust-centred life.

The Lord-centred life

In Philippians 3:3 Paul has a wonderful description of being a Christian. He defines Christians as those 'who glory in Christ Jesus'. In other words, he is suggesting that Christians are those who value Jesus more than anything or anyone else. They are those who have Jesus as their greatest love. He is at the centre of their lives. According to Paul it is our relationship with Jesus that needs to be at the heart of our Christian faith (see figure 1).

Paul starts the chapter by urging his readers to find their joy in the Lord, rather than elsewhere (3:1)

> 'Finally, my brothers, rejoice in the Lord. To write the same things to you is no trouble for me and is safe for you.'[1]

I used to think that Paul introduces the idea of 'rejoicing in the Lord' in Philippians 3:1 but then gets new wind in his sails about the dangers of legalism and lawlessness so that he changes the subject from that of rejoicing in the Lord only to pick it up again in Philippians 4:4. However, I've come to realise that that view is not correct because the theme of finding joy in the Lord is a prominent one in Paul's short letter and runs

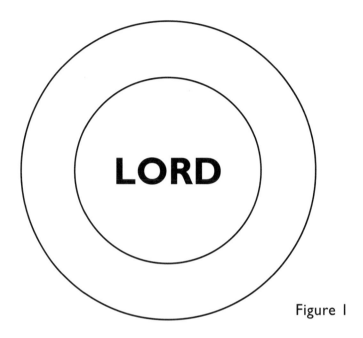

Figure I

from start to finish. That joy should be such a major theme in this letter is somewhat surprising considering that Paul is under house arrest at this time and faces the real possibility of being executed for his faith in Jesus. Paul, however, uses the word 'rejoice' nine times in Philippians and 'joy' five times. It seems unlikely that he is discarding this idea as he writes about the dangers of legalism and lawlessness.

What then does Paul mean when he repeatedly encourages the Philippians to 'rejoice in the Lord'? Is he saying that there is no place for sadness in the Christian life? Some Christians seem to suggest this. Like the chorus of the hymn 'At the cross' that concludes with the words '… and now I am happy all the day!' Is that really what Paul is promoting here? I don't believe it is. Happiness and sadness are feelings that come and go. It is not realistic to suggest that Christians (even those who regularly take note of God's grace at the cross) will feel happy all day long. That is to confuse joy with happiness. Joy is a characteristic of God's work in our lives by his Spirit (Galatians 5:22) that is independent of our circumstances. Our feelings of happiness (or not) on the other hand *are* directly related to the circumstances of our lives. In fact it is possible to be profoundly unhappy and yet profoundly joyful at the same time. I remember standing at my father's funeral service with tears tracking down my face because of the pain of my loss, but singing a wonderful hymn about Christ's victory over death. At that moment I was deeply unhappy because my father had died and yet deeply joyful about the fact that my father was with Christ for eternity.

It is also unrealistic to suggest that the Apostle himself was happy each day of his imprisonment. Here was a man who was an activist who had travelled throughout the Roman Empire with the gospel, but was now confined to four walls. Here was a man who was passionately concerned about the churches he had established but was unable to be with them. I don't believe that the apostle Paul spent each day in chains with a fixed grin. Paul is not calling the Christians in Philippi to 'smile and be happy' whatever their circumstances. He is calling them to live with Jesus at the centre of their lives. He is calling them to seek their joy in Jesus and find their strength in him so that they are able to face their life circumstances—whether it was the dangers of legalism and lawlessness or anxiety about their lives (4:6–7) or problems in the church (4:2–5) or persecution from outsiders (1:27–30).

A lot of ink has been spilt over what it is that Paul is referring to in Philippians 3:1 when he writes about repeating 'the same things' which will keep the Philippians 'safe'? Some Bible teachers have suggested that when Paul mentions here about writing 'the same things' to the Philippians he cannot be referring to 'rejoicing in the Lord' because this would have nothing to do with their safety.[2] However, I think that is precisely Paul's point here. As we'll see in a moment, the Philippians were in danger from both legalism and lawlessness and to prevent them from being plagued with these problems he calls them to actively seek their joy in the Lord, rather than elsewhere. It was in fixing their eyes on Jesus that they would be kept safe from the deadly desires of legalism and lawlessness.

Rather than being a gap in Paul's key teaching on 'rejoicing in the Lord' this section of the letter promotes the Lord-centred life as the answer to the problems of both legalism and lawlessness. Christians, Paul tells us, are to boast in Christ Jesus (v.3), they are to take joy in the righteousness that comes through faith in Christ (v.9) and they are to make it their chief ambition (like Paul) to know Christ better (v.10). In other words, they are to live conscious of the gospel day by day. When Paul tells the Philippians to 'rejoice in the Lord' he is calling them to 'live by grace'. He is telling them that a Christian life that focuses on Jesus and the gospel is one that will be kept safe from the destructive influences of legalism and lawlessness.

From time to time doctors will prescribe a preventative medicine. This is a course of treatment that will help to prevent illness, rather than cure an existing disease. This seems to be what Paul is doing here in Philippians. He is prescribing a preventative medicine. 'Rejoicing in the Lord' was the course of treatment that was required to prevent the Christians from being afflicted by legalism or lawlessness. Living with the Lord at the centre of their lives would keep them 'safe' as Christians.

The Law-centred life

Paul, however, describes two other ways of living in Philippians 3, both destructive. His first warning is of the danger of *legalism*; in other words, of Christians having 'law' at the centre of their lives (see figure 2). This was a live issue for the Philippians. Paul warns of clear and present danger in the form of 'Judaizers'. This was a group who were insisting that the Gentile Christians must become like the Jews if they wanted to be in a good relationship with God. For them *Jewish law*, rather than *faith in Jesus* needed to be at the centre of the Christian life. It was a sort of 'back to Judaism' campaign. The Christians were told that they needed to be circumcised and that they must restrict themselves to only eating certain foods in accordance with the Old Testament food laws. However, for Paul this was a different gospel, a false version of Christianity. Christians must not put *religion* or *rules* in the place of their *relationship* with God. His contention was that emphasising the law rather than finding their joy in the Lord and glorying in him was the wrong way to live.

Christians must rejoice in Christ alone and recognise that they have become Christians not because of their own obedience or their own goodness, but because of God's grace. Paul reminds us here that the important thing in Christianity is not what we *do for God* (our religious acts) but rather *knowing Christ* (our relationship with God). Obeying laws—even God's laws— is not the thing that will save us from the problem of our sin.

Paul sounds the alarm in Philippians 3:2 about the Judaizers who were misleading the Philippians: 'Watch out for those dogs, those men who do evil, those mutilators of the flesh.'

Clearly Paul wants to protect the Philippians from their destructive influence. Notice that he is not very polite in the way he describes them. He calls them '*dogs*' and he is not

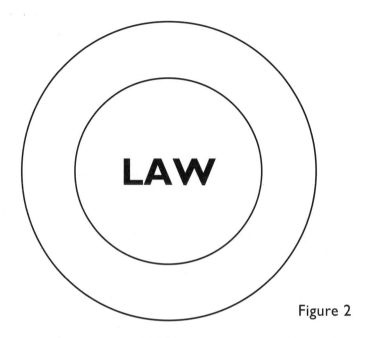

Figure 2

thinking of friendly house pets here; he is thinking about the sort of dogs that roamed the streets in packs. These were fierce feral animals which scavenged for food. He says the Judaizers were people 'who do evil'. In fact, he goes on to call them 'mutilators of the flesh'. In their desire to obey the Old Testament law and get everyone circumcised they were butchering people! Paul tells the Philippians that they don't need to be circumcised to belong to the people of God, rather they need their hearts to be transformed by God's Spirit. It was those who trusted Christ who would receive what God has promised in the Old Testament, not those who went back to slavishly obeying the Jewish law.

In Philippians 3:3 he asserts that Christians are the true 'circumcision'. In other words he is saying that Christians (whether Jews or Gentiles) are the true people of God, not those who go back to Judaism. The delight of Old Testament believers in God's law was, when rightly understood, a delight in God himself. Now *new covenant* believers have God's law etched on their hearts and minds[3] and their delight is in Jesus—the one who is the fulfilment of the law[4]. Paul says that God's Spirit is at work within Christians so that we can now have direct access to God and can worship him without the need of a tabernacle or a temple (as under the old covenant). He says that as Christians we 'worship by the Spirit of God' and we 'glory in Christ Jesus'.

In fact, Paul's own life proved that obedience to the Old Testament law did not save. If anyone could have been saved through the law, Paul could (Philippians 3:4–7). Paul had been a devout Jew. He had been circumcised according to the regulations of the Jewish law on the eighth day.[5] He was an Israelite from the tribe of Benjamin. There could be no doubt that he belonged to the Jewish people. He was 'a Hebrew of Hebrews' (3:5). On the matter of obedience to Old Testament law, he was up there with the best—Paul had been a Pharisee. In fact, he had been so committed to Judaism that he had persecuted the church. He had scrupulously obeyed God. If anyone could have become right with God through the law, it was Paul. With regard to 'legalistic righteousness' (v.6; i.e. using the law to gain acceptance with God) he had been faultless. But he had come to realise that he was bankrupt! He thought he was in credit with God because of his obedience, but what he had once considered to be profit (v.7), he now realised was loss. He had come to realise that the way he used to live was totally empty, and he had no desire to go back. He had gloried in the wrong thing. He had wasted his life by trusting in his own 'righteousness', but he had found something in Christ that he would not swap for all the righteousness of the Pharisees put together.

Paul writes (vv.8b–9): 'I consider [everything] rubbish, that I may gain Christ and be found in him, not having a righteousness of my own that comes from the law, but that which is through faith in Christ—the righteousness that comes from God and is by faith.'

Paul says that when he thinks of everything that he had once treasured, he now realised that it was smelly 'street refuse' compared to knowing Christ. In an attempt to understand the Bible I have a suggestion for you—spend some time with your rubbish this week! Open up your bin and climb on in! Welcome to the world of maggots, flies and nose-tingling smells! As you roam in your rubbish notice that the food you once took off the shop shelf doesn't look and smell quite so good anymore. Notice that you no longer want those things you once paid good money for. Spending time with your rubbish this week will give you a small idea of what Paul thought about his life before he became a Christian. He didn't want it back for a million pounds!

Paul realised that the only righteousness that counted was the righteousness that came from God through faith in Christ. He couldn't trust in anything *he* had done, only in what Christ had done for him on the cross. That single fact lies at the heart of true Christianity.

The Lust-centred life

Paul though has a second warning to sound in Philippians 3. In verses 18–19 he warns the Christians of the dangers of *lawlessness*:

'… as I have often told you before and now say again even with tears, many live as enemies of the cross of Christ. Their destiny is destruction, their god is their stomach, and their glory is in their shame. Their mind is on earthly things.'

These were people—maybe even people who professed Christianity—who had 'lust' at the centre of their lives (see figure 3). Often we associate lust with sexual desire but actually the word can be applied to our appetite for many other things too, for example our food, our clothing, our money. Paul is adamant here that this group was every bit as destructive as the Judaizers, even if their error was the polar opposite. Paul calls them 'enemies of the cross of Christ'. It seems that the Christians in Philippi were surrounded by people (as we are today) who were selfish pleasure-seekers; people who lived without any moral code. And maybe the believers were tempted to indulge in a similar lifestyle to their pagan neighbours. Maybe they felt the pressure to 'fit in' with the surrounding culture, rather than continuing to make a stand for Christ.

Paul tells the Philippians that these lawless people had the wrong focus in their lives. Instead of having their eyes fixed on a Saviour from heaven (Philippians 3:20–21), they had their minds 'on earthly things' (v.19). They lived for their appetites—their 'god [was] their stomach'—and they celebrated the very things that should have caused them shame. However, these people who seemed to live without any restraints would be held accountable by God; his punishment was coming upon them. 'Their destiny is destruction,' Paul tells the Philippians. They were headed for disaster. The Christians, in contrast, were not to live in this way. Despite the pressures of a tempting world that invited self-indulgence the Christians were not to live like non-Christians.

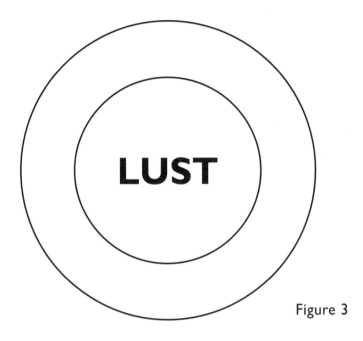

Figure 3

That is the challenge we often face as Christians today. We live surrounded by a world that tries to pull us away from Jesus. We feel the pressure to 'fit in'. We're tempted to become self-indulgent. The pressures upon us as Christians to have casual sex, to drink to excess, to overeat, to indulge in pornography, to experiment with drugs, to be greedy, to wear the best 'labelled' clothes and own the latest technology are immense. The prevailing culture is a lawless one where we are encouraged to feed our appetites. The pressures upon us today are every bit as strong as they were for the Christians in first century Philippi, and it is in this context that we need to make a stand for Christ. We need to say 'no' to these things and live a life that pleases God. But, how can we live like that? Well, only with the help of God and specifically by living in the light of the gospel. It is 'living by grace' that will help us to resist these pressures.

That is Paul's main argument here in Philippians 3. It is also what he says to Titus in Titus 2:11–12

> 'For the grace of God that brings salvation has appeared to all men. It teaches us to say "No" to ungodliness and worldly passions, and to live self-controlled, upright and godly lives in this present age ...'

It is the grace of God that teaches us to say 'no' to ungodliness and worldly passions. The answer to lawlessness (as well as legalism) is 'rejoicing in the Lord'; living day by day in the light of the gospel. That is the preventative medicine that will protect us from these deadly desires.

In the last chapter I want to explore some of the ways in which we turn as Christians to these sinful patterns of legalism and lawlessness. Sometimes we act like self-righteous Pharisees and at others we act like selfish pleasure-seeking pagans. However, an awareness of these dangers will help us to be centred on Christ once more.

Endnotes

1   English Standard Version
2   See for example the commentary on this verse by Homer A. Kent, Jr., 'Philippians,' in *The Expositor's Bible Commentary*, ed. Frank E. Gaebelein, (Grand Rapids: Zondervan, 1978; Electronic version produced by Zondervan Interactive, 2004): 'How specifically should "the same things" be understood? Surely it does not refer to the command to rejoice, for this would not have been thought to be a troublesome task or a safeguard against something dangerous.' See also the commentary by Lightfoot quoted by Ralph P. Martin in *Philippians: An Introduction and Commentary* (*Tyndale New Testament Commentaries*) (Nottingham: IVP; electronic edition, 2008): '...such an injunction [i.e. to rejoice] has no direct bearing on the safety of the Philippians.'
3   Jeremiah 31:33 c.f. Hebrews 8:10
4   Romans 10:4
5   Leviticus 12:3

7
Centred on Christ

Rejecting religion and selfish pleasure-seeking

I remember being particularly humbled as a teenager. I was at a ten pin bowling alley with my brother and two girls we were trying to impress. With a great deal of sophistication I picked up my bowling ball and headed toward the top of the alley to take my turn to release my ball and hopefully scatter the pins at the bottom. The problem was that I walked slightly too far and found myself on the highly polished surface at the top of the alley. As I swung the ball in the air, my feet disappeared from underneath me and I ended up on my backside, nursing my pride. It was not quite the impression I was trying to create!

The dangers of a slippery bowling alley, however, are nothing compared to the deadly dangers of *legalism* and *lawlessness* that the Apostle Paul warns of in Philippians 3. We must realise that these sinful patterns of living are every bit as problematic for us today as they were for the first century Christians. In fact, I want to suggest in this chapter that we all have a tendency towards one of these dangers. By nature human beings are drawn towards either legalism or lawlessness, and Christians, who are simply *rescued human beings*, bring these tendencies into their Christian lives. These wrong ways of thinking and living, however, can cause us to dethrone Jesus from the centre of our lives.

Some of us are *by temperament* legalists, others are *by temperament* lawless. Some of us sin against God by trying to rely on our performance, whilst others sin against God by pursuing our selfish passions. Some of us would make good Pharisees because we tend to be self-righteous, whereas others would make good pagans because we tend to seek our own pleasure and ignore God's laws. Some of us want to add rules to the gospel; others want to remove parts of the gospel. And being the complex human beings that we are we can be legalistic in certain areas of our lives and lawless in others. Sometimes our legalism can even be a cover for our lawlessness. An extreme example of this would be the prickly, legalistic church leader who is found to be living a double life and sleeping with prostitutes. His rule-centred façade hides his struggle with sexual sin.

Here I want to consider our Christian lives as being a bit like a pendulum that can swing from centre to the left and the right (see figure 1). When we move away from a faith focused on God's grace alone and the Jesus of the cross we can swing either to the left by embracing *lawlessness* or to the right by embracing *legalism*.[1] In sketching out what this might look like in our lives I hope we can identify the danger areas and be drawn back to a grace-centred Christianity.

The swing to the right
At the extreme of the pendulum swing to the right is nominal

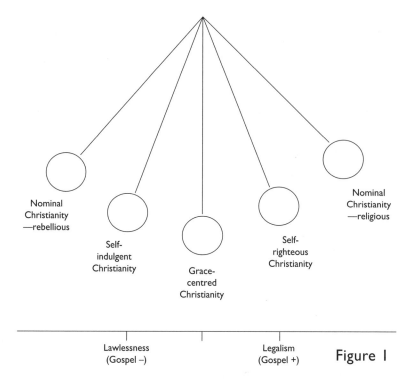

Nominal Christianity —rebellious

Self-indulgent Christianity

Grace-centred Christianity

Self-righteous Christianity

Nominal Christianity —religious

Lawlessness (Gospel −)		Legalism (Gospel +)

Figure 1

Christianity of the *religious* kind. In this position we may still call ourselves Christians but we have become detached from the gospel of God's grace because of our commitment to the rules of our religion. Maybe we turn up to church week by week to go through the rituals that we believe will cleanse us from our sin and make us right with God. Maybe we are those whose rules are so strict that we have given up on institutional Christianity altogether. When I was a pastor I met a man who sincerely believed that he was one of only a handful of genuine Christians within the UK because none of the other Christians he knew shared his unorthodox beliefs and kept his rules.

I hope that most of us will not move to such an extreme position, but the danger is always there that we incline to the right and start adding our own rules to the gospel. Some pastors control their churches by adding an extra layer of legislation about the Christian life that goes beyond the teaching of the Bible. There are rules about attendance at meetings, which clothes are acceptable, what music can be sung, how much money should be given to the church, what Christians should do with their free time etc. These churches may not have totally lost sight of God's grace, but the truth is that the good news of Jesus has been put in a strait-jacket.

Another subtle danger is that of elevating a certain 'belief system' above the gospel. My own background is reformed, and I am pleased to be associated with the doctrines that came out of the 16th century Reformation but I must never allow my reformed beliefs to become more important than my commitment to the Bible. I must be careful not to slide over and smooth out the parts of the Bible that challenge my 'belief system'. I must make sure that I am committed to the whole will of God, even when it makes me uncomfortable. Reformed doctrine (or any other 'belief system') is only useful in as far as it describes the Bible accurately. In our passion for truth we must be careful not to make reformed doctrine our central message rather than the gospel of God's grace. It never ceases to disappoint me when I meet reformed Christians who fiercely promote the 'doctrines of grace' in a manner that shows so little of this grace in their lives. Sometimes those of us who have the most to be joyful about can be the most harsh and joyless of Christians. This happens presumably because God's grace has not been truly applied in our own lives. We have a theoretical understanding of the gospel, but it has not become part of our experience in important areas of our lives.

Similar problems arise in certain sections of the charismatic church that insist on a double conversion—first to Christ and then to the charismatic movement. The same can be said of those who elevate the importance of a certain way of baptising, or a certain belief about Christ's return. In each case the 'belief system' becomes one of the defining additional features of what it means to be a Christian. It is not the gospel of God's grace alone based on the work of the cross anymore. It is a 'gospel plus' situation. Much like the Judaizers that Paul describes in Philippians 3 it is an insistence that we believe in Jesus *and* believe or do something in addition.

For some of us the danger lies in a growing smugness about our Christian lives. We start to feel that we are morally superior to others—especially those who are not Christians. We tut-tut at their behaviour and look down our noses at them. It is as if we are beginning to see what Jesus saw in us in the first place! We are happy with our religious performance. We forget that we are simply sinners saved by God's grace, and that our hearts are no better than those who surround us. We start to think that God owes us in some way. Our faithfulness in serving him should count for something, shouldn't it? That was the stance of the older son[2] in the parable of 'the Prodigal son' in Luke 15. He was disgusted that his father had welcomed his wayward younger brother home and thrown a party for him. He refused to go in. He felt his father owed him something for all his years of faithful service, but what he failed to see was that he was just as lost as his younger brother. He believed that his father's love was dependent upon his obedience, rather than freely given. That can be us too when it comes to our relationship with God. In our eyes our obedience becomes a key factor in God's acceptance of us.

The swing to the left

At the extreme of the pendulum swing to the left is nominal Christianity of the *rebellious* kind. We have become detached from the gospel of God's grace because of our commitment to personal pleasure. Although we take the label 'Christian', in fact our lives are no different to those who have no personal belief in Jesus. We've decided that our satisfaction is more important than the Christian lifestyle we are called to. We've given in to the demands of our increasingly secular society. We nurture our passions and pleasures and live rebellious, self-indulgent lives that distance us from Christ. In doing so, however, we must recognise that the Bible plainly names those who live like this 'enemies of the cross of Christ' (Philippians 3:18).[3] This is not a slight deviation from genuine Christianity but rather strikes at the heart of the true gospel.

Many of us don't take the path of open rebellion, but those of us with tendencies toward lawlessness face more subtle battles. We may have a growing admiration of the rich and famous. We read the glossy magazines (or more accurately, we look at the photos!) and we're dazzled by what we see there; we long to be like the air-brushed celebrities. We crave their care-free, money-fuelled existence which seems like heaven on earth, but we so often fail to see that their 'perfect lifestyle' is an illusion.

It's easy for us as Christians to become consumed with 'earthly things' rather than Christ. We give free reign to our appetites. We seek comfort in food, alcohol and sex, rather than Christ. We live for our favourite TV programmes, for sport, for the latest clothes and cars. Our things become all important to us in helping us to get through another day. The bitter truth is that sometimes we look no different to the unbelievers around us except that we take a quick trip to church each week. It is not that Christ is unimportant to us; it is just that we seek our pleasure and comfort elsewhere. We love many other things and we do not love the Lord our God with *all* that we are. On a day to day basis we live like those who have no regard for God's laws, and when we become aware of our sin we flippantly remind ourselves that God is a loving God and therefore that he will forgive us. We choose to forget that Christians are called to the 'obedience that comes from faith' (Romans 1:5).

Table 1 (below) gives a summary description of legalism and lawlessness and highlights some key verses from the Bible that address these sinful patterns of living.

	Legalism	**Lawlessness**
Description	Self-righteous	Self-indulgent
Emphasis	Rules	Appetite
What we need to realise about ourselves	No-one is good enough (Romans 3:23)	Christians are called to holy living (1 Peter 1:16)
What we need to realise about Christ	We can find *security* in Christ (Romans 8:28, 38–39; Philippians 1:6)	We can find *satisfaction* in Christ (Psalm 37:4: Matthew 11:28–30; 1 Peter 1:8)
Key Passage	Romans 1:17 (True righteousness is God-given)	Titus 2:11–14 (The life of grace is self-controlled)

Do you see yourself?

Do you recognise yourself here? I do. As I consider these descriptions of *legalism* and *lawlessness* I know that I'm in danger of swinging either to the right or the left, but I personally identify most with the latter. I've not taken the path of open rebellion, but I think I'm 'wired up' for lawlessness. I battle with the temptation to find my comfort in my pleasures, rather than finding my comfort in Christ and I have no doubt that this battle will rage within me until my dying day. But whether we find ourselves drifting towards either lawlessness *or* legalism let's remember the hope that is ours in the gospel. In the remainder of this chapter I want to suggest several ways in which the gospel challenges us to return to Christ. I have a message for both the legalistic Christian and the lawless Christian.

A message for the legalistic Christian

You can't earn God's forgiveness

The first thing to say to the legalistic Christian is that God's forgiveness cannot be earned. Let me tell you my own religious story. If Josh Hooker were to boast about his religion it would sound something like this. I was born into a Christian family, and I went to church from infancy. I was taught the Bible from an early age. I was baptised. I became an active church member from the age of seventeen. I have two degrees in Theology. I have been an Assistant Minister and a Minister. I am now a missionary and a Bible college lecturer. I was the Acting Principal of Namibia Evangelical Theological Seminary for four years. But it all means absolutely nothing! It all means nothing if that is what I'm putting my trust in; it means nothing without a relationship with Christ. None of those things qualify me to be a Christian. It is not faith and a little bit of religion that makes me right with God; it is faith in Christ alone. I need a Saviour.

Unfortunately, it is easy to forget that crucial fact, particularly if we have been Christians for many years. We can lose our excitement in the gospel. We can lose our first love and we can become professional church-goers, rather than people who actively trust their lives to Jesus day by day. It is true that we still attend church and play our part, but we are hiding behind our 'Christian smiles' and if the truth be told our hearts are not moved by the gospel in the way they once were. We forget that the starting point for the Christian life is not what we do for God, but rather what God has done for us. The basis of our acceptance with God is not (and never will be) how many times we go to church, the good things we do to help others, how long we spend reading our Bibles and praying, how much knowledge about God we obtain, how well-respected or senior we are in the church, or how spiritual we appear. None of those things are ever going to deal with the fatal problem of our sin. Religion does not save people—only the cross can do that. God does not accept us on the basis of what *we* do; He accepts us on the basis of what Christ has done *for us*. We cannot make ourselves Christians or even keep ourselves on that path that leads to heaven. We rely wholly on God's grace.

We need to realise that our Christian lives must be lived in the light of the cross. Ephesians 2:8–10 are fundamental verses for every Christian: 'For it is by grace you have been saved, through faith—and this not from yourselves, it is the gift of God—not by works, so that no-one can boast. For we are God's workmanship, created in Christ Jesus to do good works, which God prepared in advance for us to do.'

Paul reminds the Ephesian Christians that they are saved by God's grace. He tells them that even their ability to respond with faith is something given by God. The same is true for us. We're saved not on the basis of anything *we* do. Paul says that there is no room for boasting because we don't contribute anything. God doesn't forgive us because we're nice people or because we do good things. The Apostle is clear about the fact that *good works do not cause us to be saved.* Actually, he tells us that it is completely the other way round: *being saved causes us to do good works.* The things we do in the Christian life are not the things that earn forgiveness for us, rather they're the signs that we're saved. We are 'created in Christ Jesus to do good works, which God prepared in advance for us to do.' It was God's plan that Christians should live good lives to demonstrate the presence and reality of God's grace in our lives and bring glory to him.

Many of us find it hard to really comprehend and believe the scandal of God's grace—that Christ has done *everything* that needs to be done on the cross so that we can be saved from sin. We feel that we must contribute something either before we become Christians or after. We are therefore drawn to religion. We try to gain acceptance with God on the basis of what we do, but actually this is precisely the way in which Christianity is different from every other religion in the world. In every other religion people are trying to do something to reach God, but in Christianity God has done something to reach people. He has reached down in love by sending his son to die on a cross to deal with the problem of sin once and for all time. He has done all that needs to be done. You cannot earn God's forgiveness.

Don't lose your joy in Christ

Secondly, let me urge the legalistic Christian not to lose their joy in Christ. In Paul's letter to the Galatians he again deals with the thorny problem of the Judaizers. Because of their legalistic influence in the lives of these Christians they had lost their joy in Christ. In Galatians 4:15 he writes: 'What has happened to all your joy?'

The truth is that legalism saps our joy in Christ. We cease to delight in God and our Christianity becomes a joyless duty. But what happened to that joy in Christ we experienced on the day we first turned to Christ? Are we still filled with what the Apostle Peter calls an 'inexpressible and glorious joy' (1 Peter 1:8)? Our joy is an indicator of the state of our relationship with God. Maybe if we no longer feel that joy we have somehow swapped a living relationship for a legalistic religion. Maybe our lack of joy is a sign that we need to return to the foot of the cross once more. Jesus warns his disciples against rejoicing in their own spiritual abilities (Luke 10:17–20), but rather urges them to rejoice in God's grace: '… do not rejoice that the spirits submit to you, but rejoice that your names are written in heaven.'

Find your security in Christ, not rules

Thirdly, let me encourage the legalistic Christian to find their security in Christ. Some of us find a certain security in rules and regulations. It allows us to feel safe in a bunker of black and white when the world around us is painted in tones of grey. However Christians should not find their security in their 'obedience' to God, but rather in God himself. We need to turn again to the God who is working 'for the good of those who love him' in 'all things' (Roman 8:28), the One who will allow nothing 'in all creation' to separate us from his love 'in

Christ Jesus our Lord.' (Romans 8:39). It is Jesus himself who must be our security in an uncertain world.

We have already noted from Paul's words to the Philippians (chapter 6) that anything we do for God is faulty and can never match the perfect righteousness of Christ on offer in the gospel. The reality is that our lives (even our best thoughts and actions) are riddled with sin. No-one is good enough to please God, we have 'all sinned and fall short of the glory of God.' (Romans 3:23). And so, even as we despair of our own eternally imperfect righteousness, we rejoice in the eternally perfect righteousness of Christ given to us. We will never be able to hedge our lives with rules in such a way that we will keep sin under control, and so we need to abandon the project. What we need in the place of rules is a life of obedience motivated purely by love for God, the One who first loved us.

A message for the lawless Christian

The lawless people you envy are headed for destruction

The first thing to say to the lawless Christian is that the people you envy are headed for destruction. The New Testament writer Jude writes his letter to a church that had been infiltrated by false teachers who were promoting lawlessness[4] and he is clear about their fate. They would be convicted by God for their ungodly ways.[5] They were headed for 'the punishment of eternal fire' (Jude 7).

We must remember that the lawless people we so admire in our magazines and on our TVs will one day stand before the Lord of the universe. And the sad truth is that if they have continued serving themselves and ignoring God they will experience his righteous punishment. These people whom we hold up as role models are very often leading people astray. Their lives are empty and self-glorifying. As God's people we must not follow them.

Make sure that you do not get carried away by error

Secondly, I want to warn the lawless Christian to make sure that they don't get carried away by error. The Apostle Peter has warnings in his second letter about the influence of false teachers who promised '*freedom*' but actually were simply slaves to their own immorality.[6] Peter tells his readers to be on their guard so that they are not 'carried away by the error of lawless men and fall from [their] secure position' (2 Peter 3:17).[7] It seems that it is possible to have a taste of Christianity, but then turn away. The Bible makes it clear that this is a terrible position to be in. True faith in Jesus Christ is persevering and obedient faith. If we call ourselves Christians but continually trample on God's grace then it shows that we do not really love God as much as we say. We are treating the cross of Jesus with contempt. We must remember that our obedience to Christ is the measure of our love for him. Jesus tells his disciples just before the cross: 'If anyone loves me, he will obey my teaching' (John 14:23).

Find your satisfaction in Christ

Thirdly, let me encourage the lawless Christian to find their satisfaction in Christ. In Psalm 43:4, as the psalmist imagines worshipping God at the altar, he describes God as 'my joy and my delight'. As God's new covenant people our focus is also a place of sacrifice—not an altar, but a cross—and how much more reason we have as Christians to rejoice and delight in God as we meet him there! Like the Philippians we must: 'Rejoice in the Lord always.' (4:4)

Although we are tempted to find our satisfaction apart from God, we must seek him with all our hearts. What we long for in sex, in food, in entertainment and in possessions will never satiate our thirst. These things will always leave us longing for more, but Jesus promises 'rest' for the weary[8] and the water of life for the spiritually thirsty.[9] There is a hole in our lives that only God can fill.

Many remember the parable of the Prodigal Son[10] because of the wonderful scene that is painted for us of the father running to meet his rebellious son. However, it is interesting to note that the father does not only go out to meet the lawless younger son, he also goes out to meet the legalistic older son. Both have turned their backs on his love in different ways and have shunned him, but he seeks them both out. We must always remember that however far we run from God, whether we have embraced the legalism of the older son or the lawlessness of the younger son, God in his infinite love seeks us out to win us back to himself.

Endnotes

1   This language of swinging to the left or right is not meant to mirror the way that the same terms are used in political parlance.

2   I was recently reminded of the part of the older brother in this parable by Timothy Keller's book *The Prodigal God. Recovering the Heart of the Christian Faith* (London: Hodder & Stoughton, 2008) and noticed for the first time how the two brothers model the opposite dangers of lawlessness and legalism.

3   My thanks to Peter Ryan for pointing out to me that Paul's use of the label 'enemies of the cross of Christ' (which we might more readily associate with the idea of legalism) displays the severity of lawlessness.

4   Jude 4

5   Jude 14–15

6   2 Peter 2:19

7   See also Hebrews 6:4–6 and 10:26–31

8   Matthew 11:28–30

9   John 4:13–14

10 Luke 15:11–32

Conclusion

Living by grace

I am sure that a psychologist could draw some interesting conclusions about me from the state of my desk. My desk is rarely tidy. I tend towards a 'piling system' rather than a filing system! That is not to say that there is no order to the papers and folders you can find there; it is just that you would need to be *me* to understand where everything is. However, one extremely important piece of paper on my desk is my 'to do' list. On that paper I write down a list of jobs that need to be done, and I take great delight in striking off jobs as they are finished. Having written lists like this for many years I have discovered that not all tasks on my 'to do' list are of equal priority. Some jobs can stay on my list for a long time because they are not so important or are longer term tasks whereas others require immediate and on-going attention.

If we were drawing up a 'to do' list for our Christian lives then 'living by grace' would need to be at the top of the list. It must be our first priority. It requires immediate and on-going attention. All sorts of other priorities will vie for that position in our lives, but remembering God's grace, receiving God's grace and reapplying God's grace on a regular basis is of utmost importance for Christians. In this conclusion I want to draw together threads from each chapter of the book so that we can see what it looks like practically to 'live by grace'.

Grace Remembered

Sometimes as Christians we are inadvertently reminded of God's grace. We hear a sermon that lifts our eyes to the cross or we are moved by the reality of God's love again as we take bread and wine with our Christian brothers and sisters at a communion service. We had not personally planned to remember God's grace at these times; we simply happened upon God's grace once more in the middle of the church service. At other times we turn to God out of desperation over our sin. We mourn our wrongdoing and seek his grace because we have realised again the darkness of our hearts. At these times we confess our sins and experience God's forgiveness once more. As wonderful as those moments are, I believe that we also need to be intentional about seeking God's grace in our lives on a regular basis. The suggestion I am making in this book is that we must train ourselves to be proactive with regard to God's grace, rather than simply being reactive. We must make it a daily discipline to return in our minds to the cross of Jesus. If we fail to remember God's grace shown to us each day then our lives will not be intentionally shaped by that grace.

It was that story of grace that we looked at in the first two chapters of the book. We remembered that God the Creator intervened in history to save us from the deadly consequences of our rebellion against him. He did this by sending his Son,

Jesus, who died in our place on the cross to defeat the power of death, sin and Satan in our lives.

If you are like me you might find it easy to conjure up vague mental images of the cross and the empty grave but you find it more difficult to get fresh realisation of the importance of those history-changing moments. This is where we need help from the Bible to straighten out our thinking. It is certainly helpful to rehearse the facts of the cross in our minds as we eat our breakfast or turn them over in prayer before God as we walk to college or drive to work, but we need our thinking to be informed by God's Word if we are going to understand the glorious achievements of the first Easter. One way to do this is to memorise Bible verses that help us to focus on what Christ has done and what it means for us. Passages like Titus 3:4–7 or 1 Peter 2:24 might be helpful parts of the Bible to commit to memory and contemplate. As we read through parts of the Bible for ourselves,[1] or study the Bible to discuss it with others in a small group, we should always be asking 'What does this passage teach me about God's grace in Jesus?' At times we will need to revisit the Gospels to read an account of Christ's death, or study an Old Testament passage like Isaiah 52:13–53:12 to see how Jesus' death on our behalf is perfectly predicted there.

We can also remember God's grace by using the words of Bible-based songs and hymns. For many of us music is incredibly influential in our Christian lives. We pick up a lot of our thinking about God from the Christian songs we sing together. This is a tremendous thing if the theology is from the Bible and true and focussed on God's grace.[2] The Apostle Paul tells the Christians in Colossae: 'Let the word of Christ dwell in you richly as you teach and admonish one another with all wisdom, and as you sing psalms, hymns and spiritual songs with gratitude in your hearts to God.' (Colossians 3:16)

When I started my working life I had a forty-five minute drive to my workplace each day. This time in the car on my own gave me the opportunity to pray and to listen to sermons and Christian music. As I look back now I am profoundly grateful for those opportunities to remember God's grace in the middle of my working week. It is opportunities such as these that shape our Christian thinking.

Grace Received

In this section we were reminded from the book of Hebrews to keep our eyes on Jesus. As we daily remind ourselves of the gospel we can daily live from God's grace. Clearly, this means that we need to do more than just remember God's grace each day; it means that we must actively receive God's grace. The truth of the cross must never be a cold, bare fact in our Christian lives like something we remind ourselves of to pass a test; it must burn within us. God's grace must be responded to and applied to our own lives. This is the material that we looked at in the third, fourth and fifth chapters of the book.

In chapter 3 we saw that God's grace has brought us freedom, forgiveness, reconciliation to God, eternal life and the privilege of becoming the children of God. These are the key elements of the gospel that we need to remind ourselves of each day. We need to live in the light of these truths. These reminders of who God is and what he has done for us in Jesus will help us to get our lives in perspective. The cross has changed us forever. We are now 'in Christ'. We have been crucified with him. We can no longer live as unbelievers do thinking that we are the masters of our own destiny. We are what we are by the grace of God. This understanding will profoundly affect the way we live each day.

In chapter 4 we examined the on-going struggle that Christians face with sin (even though it is a defeated enemy) and noted two unhelpful responses to the realisation that we are sinners. The first is to live with feelings of condemnation and the second is to pretend that we no longer struggle with sin. However, an understanding of God's grace helps us to avoid these wrong ways of thinking. In chapter 5 we saw that Jesus' perfect sacrifice on the cross was the sacrifice to end all sacrifices. There is no other price to pay for sin. Jesus has dealt with its penalty once and for all time. He has removed the shame and fear associated with sin. Therefore, Christians do not need to live with condemnation for sin *because* 'there is now no condemnation for those who are in Christ Jesus' (Romans 8:1). Although sin continues to be a problem in our lives, Jesus has removed its deadly sting at the cross and God is at work within us day by day by his Spirit making us more like Jesus.

The computer I am typing at now has an 'operating system'. This is the essential computer programme that controls all the operations of my computer. If a virus attacks my 'operating system' nothing else is going to work properly. In a similar way grace must be the 'operating system' for our Christian lives. If our understanding of grace is defective or incomplete then it will adversely affect everything we do in our Christian lives. However, as we receive God's grace and grow in our understanding of God's love for us we will find the only true motivation for living a life that pleases God.

As we appreciate God's grace in our lives once more we'll naturally want to respond to God in prayer and praise for his goodness to us. Hymns and worship songs again play an important role in our Christian lives by giving us the appropriate words we need to make a joyful response to God our Saviour.

In chapter 5 we noticed that the Bible calls us not only to make a one-off response to the gospel by 'repenting and believing' (which we do when we first become Christians) but also to on-going repentance and faith. Christians must continually change their minds, and therefore their behaviour, in the light of God's present and active Kingdom. We must daily put our faith in Jesus. Repentance and faith are the two ways that we respond to God's grace in our lives.

Grace Reapplied

In chapters 6 and 7 we looked at the twin dangers of legalism and lawlessness. We saw that these were not only problems for first century Christians but are also potential problems for our lives today.

We saw in chapter 6 that the Apostle Paul uses a phrase in Philippians that explains what it means to 'live by grace'. He speaks about 'rejoicing in the Lord.' It is by actively delighting in God and his grace on a regular basis that Christians are provided with the impetus to live godly lives. 'Rejoicing in the Lord' is a preventative medicine. It protects us from the dangers of legalism and lawlessness. It is only as we revel in the wonder of the love of God for us that we are able to learn how to love God with our lives. We need to 'grasp how wide and long and high and deep is the love of Christ' (Ephesians 3:18) before we can 'live a life worthy of the calling [we] have received' (Ephesians 4:1).[3]

It is only as God's grace is regularly remembered, received and reapplied in our lives that we are able to withstand the temptations of trying to find our security in religion or our satisfaction in our pleasures. It is our daily Christian duty to delight ourselves in our God and in his grace.

The beginning at the end

As I conclude I want to take you back to the beginning of your Christian life—that time when you first understood and responded to the message of God's grace at the cross. For me it is a journey of almost three decades. My Christian life started when I was fourteen years old. I grew up in a Christian family and attended church from my first few weeks of life. Looking back now I can see how privileged I was to grow up in a stable Christian home with loving parents who taught me the Bible and prayed with me, but as I grew I struggled to know whether the things my parents believed were the things I believed. Was it real for me? Did I love Christ or was I just a church-goer from a Christian home? It was not until one Sunday evening during my teenage years that it all came into sharp focus. I realised then with blinding certainty that Christ's work on the cross was for *me*. I realised that *I* was forgiven. I was overwhelmed by emotion as I experienced God's grace in a new and unexpected way. I remember going home and trying to summon up the courage to tell my dad and mum that I had become a Christian. I remember going to bed and wondering whether I would feel differently in the morning, but then waking the next morning full of excitement about my new-found faith in Jesus. That was where the journey began for me.

I would love to tell you about my victorious and trouble-free Christian life since that time, but it has not been like that. There has, of course, been much happiness—marriage, the birth of our three children, having the privilege of teaching the Bible to others and seeing them mature in their Christian faith. However, there has also been much sadness—two lung operations as a teenager, the sudden death of my father in my early twenties, and some painful moments in my ministry as a pastor and as a Bible teacher working in Africa. Being a Christian has not exempted me from the trouble we all experience as human beings in this world, and in fact has brought some trouble of its own,[4] but being a Christian has made all the difference. I have known God's sustaining grace in the middle of laughter and tears.

Despite the fact that I have been a Christian for many years now and have also been involved in Christian ministry for most of my working life, it is important to remind myself that I am nothing more than that teenage boy. The boy who wept tears of joy as he realised that he had been forgiven by God for his sin. I must keep the beginning of my Christian life in view; that moment when I first fell at the foot of the cross and experienced God's gracious touch. I need to keep reminding myself that I am no more accepted by Christ now (or less accepted by him) after serving God as a pastor and as a missionary than I was then on that Sunday evening as the message of the cross burned in my heart for the first time.

Christians never graduate from the cross. This message of grace must remain our priority. What we were at the beginning of our Christians lives we need to be until the very end; grateful sinners who have found in Jesus forgiveness and freedom they could not find elsewhere. If we boast in anyone or anything else we have lost sight of the gospel of God's grace, which alone has transforming power and gives us a hope that lasts into eternity.

Endnotes

1   I started the book with the acknowledgement that many Christians do not take time to read God's Word regularly. It is, however, important that we develop good habits in this area. I can recommend *Explore* Bible Study notes produced by The Good Book Company and the Bible Reading Plan of Robert Murray M'Cheyne.

2   The worship music of Keith and Kristyn Getty and Stuart Townend are some of the best examples of contemporary song-writing that captures the message of God's grace. In contemporary Christian music Steven Curtis Chapman also has this emphasis.

3   Notice that Paul's letters often follow this logic of 'think right so that you can live right'. They start with breath-taking descriptions of the gospel and end with commands about how to live the Christian life. See, for example, the description of God's grace in Ephesians 1–3 followed by the application in Ephesians 4–6. It is only as we are reminded of the gospel that we are able to live in the light of it.

4   John 16:33

Further Reading

J. Bridges, *The Discipline of Grace* (Colorado Springs: Navpress, 1994)

D. A. Carson, *Scandalous. The cross and resurrection of Jesus* (Nottingham: IVP, 2010)

D. A. Carson, *The God who is there. Finding your place in God's Story* (Baker Books: Grand Rapids, 2010)

J. Chapman, *Know and tell the Gospel* (New Malden: The Good Book Company, 1998)

R. K. Hughes, *Disciplines of a godly man* (Wheaton: Crossway, 1991, Revised 2001)

T. Keller, *The Prodigal God. Recovering the Heart of the Christian Faith* (London: Hodder, 2008)

C. J. Mahaney, *Living the Cross Centred Life. Keeping the Gospel the main thing* (Colorado Springs: Multnomah, 2006)

V. Roberts, *God's big picture. Tracing the story-line of the Bible* (Leicester: IVP, 2002)

J. Stott, *The Cross of Christ.* (Leicester: IVP, 1986)